D1651891

ARBITRARY BORDERS

Political Boundaries in World History

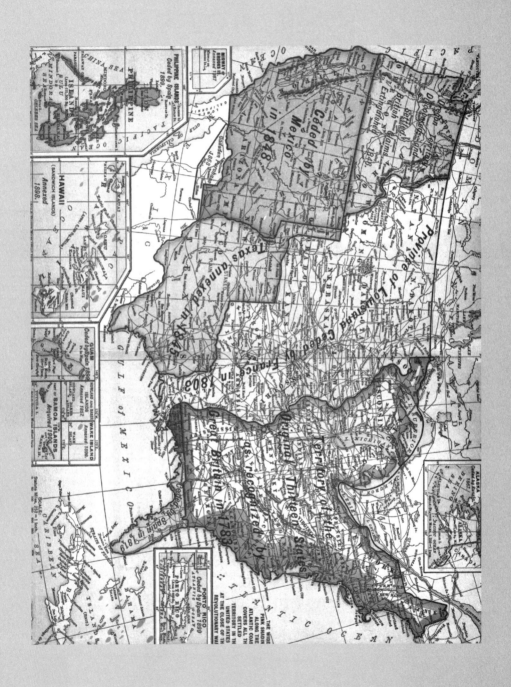

Louisiana Territory

John Davenport

Foreword by
Senator **George J. Mitchell**

Introduction by
James I. Matray
California State University, Chico

CHELSEA HOUSE
P U B L I S H E R S
A Haights Cross Communications Company
Philadelphia

08/05

FRONTIS A map of the United States and its possessions, circa 1900. The map's labels indicate the growth of territories beyond the original 13 colonies.

CHELSEA HOUSE PUBLISHERS

VP, NEW PRODUCT DEVELOPMENT Sally Cheney
DIRECTOR OF PRODUCTION Kim Shinners
CREATIVE MANAGER Takeshi Takahashi
MANUFACTURING MANAGER Diann Grasse

Staff for LOUISIANA TERRITORY

EXECUTIVE EDITOR Lee Marcott
EDITORIAL ASSISTANT Carla Greenberg
PRODUCTION EDITOR Noelle Nardone
PHOTO EDITOR Sarah Bloom
SERIES DESIGNER Takeshi Takahashi
COVER DESIGNER Keith Trego
LAYOUT EJB Publishing Services

A Haights Cross Communications ⌐ Company

www.chelseahouse.com

First Printing

9 8 7 6 5 4 3 2 1

Library of Congress Cataloging-in-Publication Data
Davenport, John, 1960-
    Louisiana Territory / John Davenport
            p. cm.
    Includes bibliographical references and index.
    ISBN 0-7910-8256-3 (hardcover)
    1. Land settlement--Louisiana--History--Juvenile literature. 2.
Frontier and pioneer life--Louisiana--Juvenile literature. 3.
Louisiana--History--Juvenile literature. 4. Missouri--History--
Juvenile literature. 5. Arkansas--History--Juvenile literature. 6.
Juvenile literature--Boundaries--Juvenile literature. I. Title.
    F369.D385 2005
    976'.03--dc22
                                                     2004027159

To Jeni for her enduring love and her inexhaustible patience—
To William and Andrew for being their father's greatest treasures
(and Judy, thanks for your sharp eyes)

Contents

Foreword

Senator George J. Mitchell

I spent years working for peace in Northern Ireland and in the Middle East. I also made many visits to the Balkans during the long and violent conflict there.

Each of the three areas is unique; so is each conflict. But there are also some similarities: in each, there are differences over religion, national identity, and territory.

Deep religious differences that lead to murderous hostility are common in human history. Competing aspirations involving national identity are more recent occurrences, but often have been just as deadly.

Territorial disputes—two or more people claiming the same land—are as old as humankind. Almost without exception, such disputes have been a factor in recent conflicts. It is impossible to calculate the extent to which the demand for land—as opposed to religion, national identity, or other factors—figures in the motivation of people caught up in conflict. In my experience it is a substantial factor that has played a role in each of the three conflicts mentioned above.

In Northern Ireland and the Middle East, the location of the border was a major factor in igniting and sustaining the conflict. And it is memorialized in a dramatic and visible way: through the construction of large walls whose purpose is to physically separate the two communities.

In Belfast, the capital and largest city in Northern Ireland, the so-called "Peace Line" cuts through the heart of the city, right across urban streets. Up to thirty feet high in places, topped with barbed wire in others, it is an ugly reminder of the duration and intensity of the conflict.

In the Middle East, as I write these words, the government of Israel has embarked on a huge and controversial effort to construct a security fence roughly along the line that separates Israel from the West Bank.

Having served a tour of duty with the U.S. Army in Berlin, which was once the site of the best known of modern walls, I am skeptical of their long-term value, although they often serve short-term needs. But it cannot be said that such structures represent a new idea. Ancient China built the Great Wall to deter nomadic Mongol tribes from attacking its population.

In much the same way, other early societies established boundaries and fortified them militarily to achieve the goal of self-protection. Borders always have separated people. Indeed, that is their purpose.

This series of books examines the important and timely issue of the significance of arbitrary borders in history. Each volume focuses attention on a territorial division, but the analytical approach is more comprehensive. These studies describe arbitrary borders as places where people interact differently from the way they would if the boundary did not exist. This pattern is especially pronounced where there is no geographic reason for the boundary and no history recognizing its legitimacy. Even though many borders have been defined without legal precision, governments frequently have provided vigorous monitoring and military defense for them.

This series will show how the migration of people and exchange of goods almost always work to undermine the separation that borders seek to maintain. The continuing evolution of a European community provides a contemporary example illustrating this point, most obviously with the adoption of a single currency. Moreover, even former Soviet bloc nations have eliminated barriers to economic and political integration.

Globalization has emerged as one of the most powerful forces in international affairs during the twenty-first century. Not only have markets for the exchange of goods and services become genuinely worldwide, but instant communication and sharing of information have shattered old barriers separating people. Some scholars even argue that globalization has made the entire concept of a territorial nation-state irrelevant. Although the assertion is certainly premature and probably wrong, it highlights the importance of recognizing how borders often have reflected and affirmed the cultural, ethnic, or linguistic perimeters that define a people or a country.

Since the Cold War ended, competition over resources or a variety of interests threaten boundaries more than ever, resulting in contentious interaction, conflict, adaptation, and intermixture. How people define their borders is also a factor in determining how events develop in the surrounding region. This series will provide detailed descriptions of selected arbitrary borders in history with the objective of providing insights on how artificial boundaries separating people will influence international affairs during the next century.

Senator George J. Mitchell
October 2003

Introduction

James I. Matray
California State University, Chico

Throughout history, borders have separated people. Scholars have devoted considerable attention to assessing the significance and impact of territorial boundaries on the course of human history, explaining how they often have been sources of controversy and conflict. In the modern age, the rise of nation-states in Europe created the need for governments to negotiate treaties to confirm boundary lines that periodically changed as a consequence of wars and revolutions. European expansion in the nineteenth century imposed new borders on Africa and Asia. Many native peoples viewed these boundaries as arbitrary and, after independence, continued to contest their legitimacy. At the end of both world wars in the twentieth century, world leaders drew artificial and impermanent lines separating assorted people around the globe. Borders certainly are among the most important factors that have influenced the development of world affairs.

Chelsea House Publishers decided to publish a collection of books looking at arbitrary borders in history in response to the revival of the nuclear crisis in North Korea in October 2002. Recent tensions on the Korean peninsula are a direct consequence of Korea's partition at the 38th parallel at the end of World War II. Other nations in human history have suffered because of similar artificial divisions that have been the result of either international or domestic factors and often a combination of both. In the case of Korea, the United States and the Soviet Union decided in August 1945 to divide the country into two zones of military occupation ostensibly to facilitate the surrender of Japanese forces. However, a political contest was then underway inside Korea to determine the future of the nation after forty years of Japanese colonial rule. The Cold War then created two Koreas with sharply contrasting political, social, and economic systems that symbolized an ideological split among the Korean people. Borders separate people, but rarely prevent their economic, political, social, and cultural interaction. But in Korea, an artificial border has existed since 1945 as a nearly impenetrable barrier precluding meaningful contact between two portions of the same population. Ultimately, two authentic Koreas emerged, exposing how an arbitrary boundary can create circumstances resulting even in the permanent division of a homogeneous people in a historically united land.

Korea's experience in dealing with artificial division may well be unique, but it is not without historical parallels. The first set of books in this series on arbitrary boundaries will provide description and analysis of the division of the Middle East after World War I, the Iron Curtain in Central Europe during the Cold War, the United States-Mexico border, the 17th parallel in Vietnam, and the Mason-Dixon Line. A second set of books will address the Great Wall in China, the Green Line in Israel, and the 38th parallel and demilitarized zone in Korea. Finally, there will be volumes describing how discord over artificial borders in the Louisiana Territory, Northern Ireland, and Czechoslovakia reflected fundamental disputes about sovereignty, religion, and ethnicity. Admittedly, there are many significant differences between these boundaries, but these books will strive to cover as many common themes as possible. In so doing, each will help readers conceptualize how complex factors such as colonialism, culture, and economics determine the nature of contact between people along these borders. Although globalization has emerged as a powerful force working against the creation and maintenance of lines separating people, boundaries likely will endure as factors having a persistent influence on world events. This series of books will provide insights about the impact of arbitrary borders on human history and how such borders continue to shape the modern world.

James I. Matray
Chico, California
April 2004

1

Looking at
Louisiana

Thomas Jefferson knew that the common folk wrote to him because they believed their president was a man of the people. Although his schedule as the young nation's chief executive contained little spare time, Jefferson always found a free moment to read the letters written by average Americans and sent to the capital postage paid. He read each and every letter. The contents of individual letters ranged from fairly sophisticated commentaries on public policy to mundane requests from writers who imagined the chief executive had a sympathetic ear. No matter what the subject, Jefferson's correspondents had a lot to say.

On this particular morning in 1805, the president's stack of incoming mail included a letter from a middling planter struggling to get by in Bourbon County, Kentucky. Alexander Ogle had chosen his words carefully as he put pen to paper. He wrote deferentially to Jefferson that even though he was "a Stranger," he had the "highest Respect" for his country's leader. The Kentuckian went on to apologize for troubling such an important man "with this Scrawl," but he had an urgent request and hoped that Jefferson would "have it in his Power and be Pleased" to grant it.[1] Ogle recounted for the president how three years earlier he had "adventured to send three Boatloads of Flour to New Orleans." Due to the cargo being "a little damaged ... the Glut of the Market then and the Caprice of the Spaniards who were then in possession of that place," this initial venture turned out to be less than profitable. Here Ogle got straight to the point—he had decided to "seek my Fortune in the Louisiana Country."[2] Material success was assumed to be within the reach of every American, something of a birthright in fact. Dreams came true for the honest, industrious man; Ogle just needed a bit of assistance in realizing his dream. A letter of introduction from Jefferson, Ogle concluded, to "some of your Friends there" would make purchasing good farmland all the easier for the strapped but optimistic Kentucky planter.[3] The Louisiana Territory offered hope and abundant land to a farmer whose fortunes had stalled through no fault of his own.

A portrait of President Thomas Jefferson, by Rembrandt Peale, 1800. Jefferson believed that America had a God-given mission to spread republican government and democracy to all parts of North America, and the Louisiana Purchase fit into his grand plan of expansion and development for the country.

History does not record how Jefferson responded to Ogle's petition nor does it say how the president dealt with a slightly different request from one James Law of Somerset County, New Jersey. Law also had his eye on a future in Louisiana but with aims that were quite different from Ogle's. Twenty-six years old, Law suffered through a tedious existence as a mere country schoolteacher when, in reality, he longed, like every good America, "to attain to something greater."[4] Jefferson, Law confidently felt, could help him in this ambition. Using the creative spelling common in the days before compulsory public education, Law pled his case: "By the Late traty with France I suppose there will be a Number of young men who may get into imploy in the Louisiana Country ... Perhaps Sir I might be capable of acting in some of them places to the advantage of [the] Country."[5] Law, to put it bluntly, wanted a job, a secure job with the government, working for the progress of the newly acquired Louisiana Territory. Louisiana held out the promise of a career to a young man suffocating in the close confines of a musty schoolhouse.

Ogle, Law, and Jefferson looked at the same place and saw very different things. Ogle envisaged land—open, empty land—ready to be settled, tamed, and put under the plow. Law perceived a place desperately in need of organization and administration at the hands of a new breed of forward-looking Americans. The president, for his part, surveyed in his imagination a vast natural expanse that had to be explored, mapped, and absorbed into an American nation that he conceived of as an "empire of liberty."[6] Jefferson believed deeply in the notion that America had a God-given mission to spread republican government and democracy to all parts of North America, beginning with the wild open spaces of the West.

The three Americans looked at the Louisiana Territory, and each saw exactly what he wanted, needed, and hoped to see. Still, in a strange sense, these men together viewed Louisiana as only Americans could. One envisaged a wholesome, honest relationship with the land; his opposite number had an understanding of the territory as a young place suited to the energy and initiative of young men. The president thought in terms of a national project to expand the boundaries of liberty and freedom. Within a historical context, however, people had been inventing and reinventing the Louisiana Territory as they saw fit for millennia before the trio above had even thought about it.

The region's broad rivers, grassy plains, and towering mountains, of course, had no part in such exercises of the imagination; they stood mute from the Gulf of Mexico to the Canadian border, much as they always had done. Nature had no purpose other than being. The landscape retained its ancient contours, oblivious to the fanciful flights of the human mind. Artificial lines appeared nowhere on the ground. The only "borders" the unin-habited Louisiana Territory had were those put there by time itself—borders of water, rock, and soil. Human minds, however, from those of the earliest Native Americans to those of settlers trying to scratch a living from the tough sod of the plains, made a habit of overlaying, and thus altering, the land with their per-ceptions, ideas, dreams, hopes, and fears. People looking at Louisiana changed it with their very gaze, making it a place at once real and imagined.

Successive groups of people, beginning with the Native Americans, saw in the mute landscape resources to be used, then political creations to be controlled, and finally ideas to be fought over. At each stage of development, the "Louisiana" that people imagined drew farther away from the real place, increasingly becoming a mental fixture. Transforming the land from some-thing real into an abstraction was no easy task; it was hard to turn raw nature into a concept. The process began with the dif-fering agendas of those observing it, but its successful comple-tion hinged on coming up with ever-more abstract imagery through which the land could be given meaning. At first, this meant associating it with distinct lifeways and cultural patterns; later, Louisiana became a political entity. Finally, the territory was incorporated into a national ideology that raised it to the highest level of abstraction. Culture and politics continued to play their parts at this stage, but Louisiana blurred into an idea. In each instance, the borders that people drew changed not on the ground itself, where nature's boundary lines were indelibly etched, but in the human minds and on the maps that changed objective physical forms into subjective features.

All borders are human fabrications, utterly arbitrary, and always shifting with this or that social, cultural, or political wind. They are indispensable, because they plainly mark out the geo-graphical object being viewed by a particular set of human sub-jects while establishing the terms in which it will be viewed. Borders tell the observer, in other words, what she or he is look-ing at and how it might be imagined. The only real distinction is in the extent to which a border marks out a relationship to the natural world. Some boundary lines identify more concrete connections to the real world than others. Thus the relative level of abstraction is paramount when discussing how people choose to partition the land.

So it was with the Louisiana Territory. Like so many other places around the world, the Louisiana Country, as it was called in Jefferson's day, did not exist outside of the minds of those looking at it, and each successive group took an interest in what they thought they saw there. Native Americans viewed the land as one massive support system that sustained them and animated their way of life. Their borders, as a result, reflected local survival strategies. Lacking political states and national ideologies, Native Americans imagined fluid lines between language and cultural groups, each with a mode of existence within and dependent upon the natural world, which moved as the people did. Their borders served as an extension of a specific set of lifeways and interpretive systems that together constituted a culture. The boundaries of the Louisiana Territory, for Native Americans, took form as cultural constructs predicated upon tangible bonds with nature.

European empire builders, whether French, Spanish, or English, on the contrary, saw the Louisiana Territory as a fixed buffer zone that functioned as a political necessity. European politics, consequently, created the borders that defined it. The place was, in effect, a transitional space whose borders established where the influence of one empire ended and where that of its neighbor began. Louisiana's political boundaries became ramparts, sometimes ridiculously porous, but ramparts nonetheless.

Europeans looked at Louisiana and thought that they saw bold imperial map lines that they could use to keep the competitive "other" at arm's length. Participants in the European struggle to build and maintain extensions of their respective empires in North America glared at each other across a swath of land that none might have particularly wanted but none were willing to

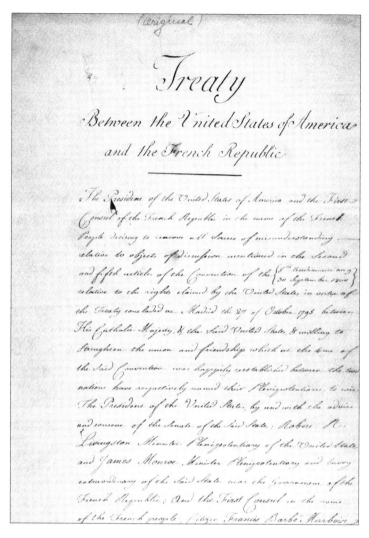

The American original of the Louisiana Purchase, signed on April 30, 1803, which ceded France's Louisiana Territory to the United States for $15 million. With the signing of this document, the United States nearly doubled in size, and President Thomas Jefferson obtained much more land than he had originally estimated.

surrender without a good deal of the intrigue for which the courts of Europe were famous. Except in the sense of the natural resources that might be extracted, the European border imagery differed substantially from the Native American imagery it replaced. Imperial mapmakers gave only a cursory glance in the direction of the natural world. The lines they drew generally conformed to nature's borders only in the sense that they tended to follow the contours of mountain ranges and rivers. They reflected political rather than cultural formations. The French and the Spanish perceived no linkages between themselves and the land apart from its value in the larger scheme of global dynastic competition. The level of abstraction inherent in Europeans borders stood in sharp contrast to the more concrete boundaries of Native Americans.

The citizens of the new United States who took final possession of the land turned out to have perhaps the most complex vision of the Louisiana Territory. Nature and the physical reality of the land could not be ignored by a people still overwhelmingly employed in agricultural pursuits. Cultural imperatives similarly played a part in the process of cobbling together a view of the Louisiana Territory that harmonized with American society and institutions. Moreover, the rush to organize the territory politically, soon after its acquisition in 1803, demonstrates clearly that its projected borders were already being conceived of as national boundaries. In these ways, the American phase of the area's development appears at first to be more synthetic than novel. One could argue that the American model symbolized the next logical evolutionary stage, a blending of earlier models. The difference, however, came in the ideological impulse behind the purchase and occupation of Louisiana.

The notion that the land stood as little more than empty space, vacant property to be settled and brought under the plow by honest hardworking American farmers, operated in tandem with an abiding belief in a God-given mission to extend the United States to the Pacific. Borders, for Americans, became symbols of a national experiment that would reshape North America. The nation's manifest destiny lay in the creation of an all-encompassing, continental republic. Americans would most certainly fight their share of battles, often against each other, to decide the cultural and political orientation of the Louisiana

Territory, but in the end, it was ideas that mattered. Previous mindsets and perspectives had no role in this progression; the American mission transcended them and dictated their erasure. Perhaps more than anything else, this fact demonstrated that the process of imagining the physical place called Louisiana reached its zenith in the United States phase. The most abstract of all the developmental arrangements up to that point, the national period produced the Louisiana Territory's most arbitrary borders. They were based almost exclusively on what people thought and felt.

Whether Alexander Ogle or James Law ever found what they were after in the Louisiana Territory is a question whose answer is lost in time. Jefferson, who never dreamed of acquiring the entire place anyway, is another story; in the end, he most certainly got what he wanted. The third president's "empire of liberty" moved that much closer toward realization with the purchase of Louisiana in 1803. In fact, the United States nearly doubled in size, and the notion of an America stretching from the Atlantic to the Pacific no longer seemed farfetched. A continental democracy might be just around the corner. The region would first have to be explored, of course. Then would come the maps, the settlers, the merchants, the towns, the states, and the exploitation—in short, modernity. Arbitrary borders gave the entire exercise form and an internally logical structure.

The Louisiana Territory moved from one mental construct and set of borders to another during its history. The Indians had theirs; the European empires had theirs; finally, the citizens of the United States inserted their own set. Despite all this human commotion, however, the place remained, now a spectator to its own fictional dismemberment. The rivers flowed; the grasses swayed in the wind; the mountains sat majestically. The actual piece of North America that was the Louisiana Territory barely noticed as its imaginary self rose, fell, and then rose again in the minds of this or that group of people. Nature did not pay attention to the men and women who altered the Louisiana Territory, over and over, just by looking at it.

2

Nature's Borders

The area that once made up the Louisiana Territory is a vast piece of real estate that begins at the delta of the mighty Mississippi River and then balloons northward in the direction of modern-day Nebraska and Iowa before sweeping to the west into what are today the states of Montana and Wyoming. The entire region encompasses all or part of thirteen states, seven major rivers, and two time zones; it sprawls out over a land mass roughly the size of Alaska. This unique place is, with good reason, called America's heartland.

Nature gave the Louisiana Territory dramatic and very real borders that defined climatic zones, plant and animal habitats, and hydrological complexes. The territory's boundaries held within them geophysical and ecological structures that differed substantially from those in the regions that lay to the east and west. These were borders in the truest sense of the word, genuine markers identifying and separating a singular physical space from its neighbors. Millions of years in the making, these dividing lines were anything but arbitrary.

The Mississippi River, in all its languid majesty, flowed along the Louisiana Territory's eastern edge. The Rocky Mountains rose up as a barrier in the west. To the south lay the beautiful but desolate scrubland that punctuated the region's grassy expanses in its lower parts. Where the territory reached its southernmost extreme, pine forests, bayous, and marshlands dominated the landscape as it merged into the Gulf of Mexico. Within this cup-shaped enclosure sat a gently waving sea of grass, cut through here and there by lacy blue ribbons that funneled incredible quantities of water into the Mississippi-Missouri river system. Indeed, taken as a whole, the Louisiana Territory functioned as one massive drainage basin pointed toward the Mississippi and the sea.

Beginning as a mere trickle in the far north, water flowed, as it does now, relentlessly southward. Creeks, streams, and tributaries merged to form a giant web of waterways that stretched across 1,244 square miles of North America, at the same time draining water from a staggering 1.2 million square miles of territory.[7]

Leaves along the Mississippi River glisten in the morning sun. The mighty river flows from Canada to the Gulf of Mexico—its entire system of waterways draining water from 1.2 million square miles of land. It served as a convenient boundary for the eastern edge of the Louisiana Territory.

Today, the average discharge rate of the broader river formation, which includes the Mississippi, Missouri, Platte, and Red rivers, is an astounding 611,000 cubic feet of water per second. In the past, this discharge rate was even greater. At one time in the history of this regal watercourse, approximately 400 million metric tons of nutrient-laden sediment clouded these waters each year, guaranteeing that the adjacent flood plain was covered over with a thick layer of dark, rich topsoil.[8] Later observers could not help but notice the rich loam that characterized the rivers' shores. Meriwether Lewis, during his famous 1804–1806 expedition with William Clark, described the river margins as being "uniformly fertile consisting of a dark loam intermixed with a proportion of fine sand."[9] In this fertile ground, plants grew in abundance, drawing in birds, mammals, fish, and insects of infinite variety. The water brought and kept life.

Even where the rivers did not penetrate, nature provided. The trees that lined the banks of the area's major rivers needed the cool abundance of a riparian environment; the stout grasses of the Great Plains, by contrast, were far less choosy. Tall and short grasses covered the seemingly limitless prairies. Historically, over 80 million acres of tall grass and 20 million acres of short grass overspread the Louisiana Territory.[10]

Able to withstand the broiling summers and frigid winters common to their home, the grasses grew so densely that their root systems merged to form an almost impenetrable, interlocking mat of sod. So vast, in fact, were the grasslands that one could, with only occasional interruptions, walk from Canada to Texas without leaving their green-amber precincts. An early visitor to the prairie sea in the nineteenth century remarked that he "could see nothing in any direction but sky and grass"[11] Had he taken a second look, this tourist might have noticed some of the 3,067 different species of flowers that shared the land with the grasses.[12]

The steppes of the future Louisiana Territory possessed abundant grasses and exquisite soil but suffered from a fickle climate prone to extremes. Temperatures ranged from well below zero in the depths of winter to over 90°F in summer. Fierce wind-blown blizzards raked the plains, bringing snow and ice. A few short months later, violent thunderstorms and tornadoes swept across the land, dropping torrents of rain. In addition to these summertime deluges, electrical storms accompanied by crackling lightning often ignited the tinder-dry prairie grass, creating infernos that blackened thousands of acres at a time. One later traveler waxed poetic as he recalled watching prairie fires roll "like breakers of the sea upon the dried grass [sweeping] it in a wave of fire from the ground."[13]

Such blazes replenished the soil and promoted the growth of fresh, young grass. Fire, in short, rejuvenated the plains. For the resident animals, however, prairie flames meant certain death for the old, the sick, or the slow. As a modern natural historian has pointed out, flocks of scavenging birds "followed the fires, consuming the charred remains of those caught in the conflagration."[14] The forces of the natural world took away life with as much impartiality as they gave it. The seasons brought curses as well as blessings.

THE GREAT PLAINS TODAY

The swaying grasses that once blanketed the Louisiana Territory have long since disappeared from most of their former range. Beginning in earnest in the 1870s, farmers tore through the tough prairie sod with their steel plows, ripped out the native grasses by the roots, and planted in their stead wheat, corn, barley, and any number of other domesticated cereal crops. By the early twentieth century, the old Louisiana Territory had become the breadbasket of the world. Even after the disastrous droughts and dust storms of the 1930s, the region remained a globally important grain producer, with crop yields and general output increasing each decade. Nature gave its bounty to the farmers of the Great Plains, and continued to provide through the years.

The human story is a bit different. With the exception of Denver and the river cities of St. Louis, Des Moines, Kansas City, and New Orleans, the region never really urbanized, nor did it develop the kind of commercial-industrial base that comes with urbanization. Economic diversity was limited, and this caused a peculiar demographic stagnation. Regional growth stalled. By the end of the twentieth century, the population of the Plains began to decline, and the pattern continues today. Crops grown on family farms represent a smaller percentage of agricultural production than ever before; young people are leaving not only the farms on which they grew up but entire states. From Kansas to the Dakotas, population levels are declining at rates approaching 10 to 20 percent while the median age rises. Towns are, in some cases, literally being abandoned. It has been said that the "region has been experiencing a culture shock."[*] One positive effect of this downward progression had been a new appreciation for the natural splendor of the region. As Rob McKim, the vice president of the Nature Conservancy, has recently noted, "People are leaving small towns, communities are declining, and the depopulation of the Great Plains is accelerating... So now people are looking at buffalo grazing, ecotourism, and other ways to conserve and restore what once was the American Serengeti."[**]

[*] John G. Mitchell, "Change of Heartland: America's Rural Interior Searches for New Horizons," *National Geographic*, (May 2004), p. 8.

[**] Stephen Kinzer, "American Prairie Overlooked No More," *New York Times*, June 24, 2004, A14.

Along the eastern boundary of the Louisiana Territory, nature passed a gentler hand. The climate here, while often hard, was less unruly than on the open grasslands. Here, forests of maple in the north gave way to dense stands of hickory and oak through what is now Missouri and Arkansas. A mixed forest of hardwoods and pine rose out of the clay-rich yellow soil of the lower Mississippi near the river's terminus.

These virgin forests hugged the shoreline of an ancient Mississippi River that carried three times as much water as any other river in North America.[15] Wide, slow moving, and muddy, the Mississippi spanned the entire length of the Louisiana Territory from north to south. The broad river functioned as a concrete natural boundary, marking the transition from the humid and hilly eastern woodlands to the relatively dry, flat plains. What the Mississippi delineated existed in the hard, quantifiable worlds of geology, biology, and climate. Before human minds transformed it into an idea, the great river was one of nature's premier borders.

Far across the sprawling prairie, in the direction of the setting sun, the land climbed gently, often imperceptibly, toward the majestic Rocky Mountains. A true continental divide, the Rockies ranged in elevation up to 14,000 feet, many parts remaining snow-covered year round. One link in a mountain chain that formed the topographic spine of North America, the Rockies separated the Great Basin and the far West from the Plains region. Every bit as formidable a barrier as the Mississippi, the Rocky Mountains once lay on the floor of a shallow inland sea that took up the middle of the continent 340 million years ago.

Torn apart and reassembled over the ages by a combination of erosion, plate tectonics, and volcanic activity, the mountains sat brooding over a thousand miles of horizon. The thick montane forests, alpine meadows, and snowy peaks of the Rockies contrasted sharply with the more desert-like mountains to the west and the plains to the east. Much like the Mississippi, the Rocky Mountains physically and absolutely demarcated the Louisiana Territory.

Mountains, prairies, and rivers gave literal form to a place that was home to an astonishing array of birds, mammals, fish, and insects. The land teemed with life. Migratory birds filled the skies during those seasons when they followed the ancient flyways north and south. Although the birds avoided flying over the most open stretches of grassland, preferring to the better-wooded and well-watered periphery, the grand flocks at times blotted out the sun with millions of pairs of wings. Songbirds of all kinds added their numbers to the migratory horde as did nesting shorebirds. To this day, 40 percent of the birds in North America use the territory as their principal flyway.[16] At the pinnacle of the avian food chain, hawks, eagles, and falcons prowled among the clouds, lending their lethal grace and beauty to the tableaux of life. The Louisiana Territory, long before the Europeans arrived, indeed before any humans had drifted in at all, claimed one of the largest concentrations of birds in North America.

Grazing beneath these bird-filled skies was a multitude of beasts, most famously the enormous herds of the region's signature animal, the North American bison. The last remnant of the prehistoric creatures known as the megafauna, the buffalo dominated the grassland. An estimated 50 million buffalo shook the plains with their thunderous hooves before Europeans arrived in the region. The herds were mind-boggling in sheer size; single herds reportedly stretched for miles. At one point in time, the buffalo covered nearly 400,000 square miles with their massive bulk.[17] Chomping their way lazily across prairies humming with the sounds of an estimated 10 million insects per acre,[18] the buffalo shared their Louisiana Territory home with other animals soon to achieve almost iconic status in American history.

Grizzly bears stomped through the Rocky Mountains and beyond, bringing down elk and snatching fish from icy, crystal-clear streams. These gargantuan yet agile omnivores could be found throughout the northern and central plains where they competed with wolves for the title of top predator. Meriwether Lewis found the grizzly to be a "furious and formidable

Bison graze on native prairie grasses in Missouri, much as they did at the time of the Louisiana Purchase. In the 1800s, though, the enormous herds stretched for miles, dominating the grasslands. Buffalo are the last descendants of the prehistoric creatures known as the megafauna.

anamal," whereas wolves amazed him by being "extreemly fleet and dureable."[19]

For all their fearsome splendor, the grizzly and the wolf never matched the humble beaver in terms of being associated with the Louisiana Territory. Rivers, especially those nearest the Rockies, very rarely ran their course without at some point being interrupted by a beaver dam. These ingenious and industrious rodents are believed to have numbered anywhere from 60 to 400 million in the period before European contact. Entire stands of trees fell to the gnawing incisors of the many eager builders as they constructed their dams and dens. So formidable were their engineering skills that rivers often changed course, their flow of water altered. Lewis and Clark marveled at the sight of "a tree nearly 3 feet in diameter that had been felled by them."[20]

This veritable riot of life in an awesome landscape lay within borders that functioned as such in the purest sense of the term.

Nature's borders defined physical space and organic relationships that had real form. They served as concrete borders that divided the continent. Climatic zones, rocks, rivers, plants, and animals—there is nothing arbitrary about these. It can be argued, therefore, that the only true borders the Louisiana Territory ever possessed existed in the absence of human imagination. After that, the region's borders drifted slowly away from a basis in the natural world toward abstraction. Once people arrived, the incremental process of drawing arbitrary lines began.

The transition from a material to a mental bordering of the Louisiana Territory got underway long ago. Somewhere approximately 20 millennia ago, the ancestors of the Native Americans, people known as the paleo-Indians, became the first residents of the place to see, experience, and imagine the land. Emerging through glacial passages that opened up as the earth began to warm its way out of the last ice age, these hardy migrants cast their eyes to the south and saw Louisiana.

3

The
Indian Way

The earliest immigrants to the Louisiana Territory were the ancestors of the Native Americans, people who wandered in from northern Asia some 15,000 to 20,000 years ago. Their long journey began in Siberia and was made possible by a combination of nature's good graces and human ingenuity. People devised the methods by which they could populate an entirely new continent, but nature provided the means for basic survival. The land and its occupants evolved together, developing over time a balanced, infinitely flexible working relationship. The descendents of these earliest sojourners came to have a unique perspective on the place that gave them the gift of life. Native Americans looked on the Louisiana Territory as a closed support system, a complex of timeless yet ever-changing and often unpredictable natural cycles that very simply allowed them to exist. When they constructed borders between themselves, those boundaries matched the fluidity of their traditional circumstances. Native American borders, in other words, flowed and fluxed with the very real natural resource base the people depended upon. In this, they embodied a concreteness that later human dividing lines lacked. This was the Indian way.

The last of the great ice ages concentrated so much seawater in the earth's polar caps and glaciers that ocean levels plummeted all around the globe. Towering sheets of ice smothered most of the Northern Hemisphere, altering the topography of whole continents. One result of this big freeze was the exposure of the seafloor across the narrow strait separating Asia from North America. Falling sea levels had the effect of pushing up the land, essentially creating a bridge between the landmasses. Known as today as Beringia, in reference to the Bering Strait it once spanned, this stretch of flat, low-lying ground became a highway of sorts for animals and humans, a gateway into another world.

Coming across the land bridge in small groups, following the animal herds that they hunted, the paleo-Indians took advantage of the opportunity to cross over into an uninhabited continent teeming with wildlife and rich in the raw materials of life. With no conveyances other than their own leather-shod feet or perhaps small, primitive boats, these first Americans moved slowly into modern Alaska. Over the course of hundreds of generations, they meandered southward, negotiating the narrow passages that periodically opened up between the Canadian ice sheet and the Pacific Ocean. Keeping the glaciers on their left and the sea on their right, the paleo-Indians trekked to the south until they turned east to reach the vast interior of the continent.

Some of the compatriots of these overland migrants chose a different route to their new home. These people shunned the land bridge in favor of the faster and less rigorous, if somewhat more dangerous, journey by boat. Hugging the shoreline for what safety they could get, these ancient mariners paddled down the coast, eventually settling as far south as modern Chile. The camps they established along the way served as bases for inland excursions that augmented the land migrations. By boat and by foot, North America gained new tenants who came to rest, after millennia of steady movement, on the grasslands, along the rivers, and in the mountain forests of what would be the Louisiana Territory.

Little is known for certain about the culture these prehistoric settlers brought with them as they fanned out across the plains, along the rivers, and through the woodlands. What precious little can be ascertained about their lifeways comes from the tools they left behind, namely spearheads of varying designs, shapes, and sizes. Dated with some confidence to anywhere from 7,000 to 11,000 years before the present, these remarkably sophisticated and exquisitely crafted blades bespeak a hunting-oriented cultural tradition. Animal flesh provided the paleo-Indians with a protein-rich diet that was supplemented with fruit, nuts, and tubers gathered from local plants and trees.

No doubt daily life in the prehistoric Louisiana Territory revolved to a large degree around the chase and slaughter of the megafauna that stomped around North America until about 9,000 years ago. The gargantuan browsing and grazing animals included such well-known species as mammoths, mastodons, wooly rhinos, giant ground sloth, and huge bison. From these creatures, the paleo-Indians took the meat, hides, bones, and sinew that allowed them to flourish. The nearly inexhaustible supply of game encouraged these nomadic hunters to kill their quarry with abandon. In a single day about 8,000 years ago, for instance, a party of ancient hunters in Colorado dispatched and butchered over 200 buffalo, taking back to their camp an estimated 8,000 pounds of meat and skin, a bounteous haul by any measure.[21]

Unfortunately for the paleo-Indians, the halcyon days of megafauna hunting did not last forever. Most likely, a combination of severe hunting pressure and climate change, both perhaps aggravated by epidemic disease, caused the oversized species that greeted the first immigrants to disappear. Their demise forced the humans who depended upon them to adapt, and hunter-gatherers had to reverse the order of their occupations. All over the continent, scattered groups began to favor gathering over hunting, indirectly leading them to cultivate crops and adopt a more sedentary lifestyle. As early Indians shifted toward a reliance on agriculture, or at least took up part-time farming, their societies became more stable and highly differentiated. Even those groups that maintained a primary focus on hunting had to change, developing traditions and assumptions based on specific target species, most famously the buffalo. These buffalo hunters regularly interacted with and often fought with their farming neighbors as each began to construct boundaries to define themselves and the opposite "others." Over time, the first Native Americans came, as one writer has put it, "to live within chosen areas."[22] Those "chosen areas" required borders.

In short, long before the first Europeans crossed the Mississippi into the Louisiana Territory, the native inhabitants were diverging along lines dictated by differing interests and agendas. As the centuries passed, according to the historian Gary Nash, "myriad ways of life had developed" among the Native Americans well before "Europeans found their way to the very old 'New World.'"[23] Some modern historians and anthropologists have even argued that the gulf between agriculturists and hunters was so wide that "the Great Plains cultural area" should be "treated as two different areas."[24] Whether 2, 20, or 200, disparate groups of Native Americans adopted unique ways of interacting with the land and drew borders to set themselves apart from their neighbors.

Limited by the tough prairie sod and the absence of natural irrigation, the agriculturists farmed fields established around permanent or semi-permanent villages along the territory's great rivers. The Arikara, Mandan, and Hidatsa were among those who tilled the soil in the north; further south the farming folk included the Wichita, Osage, and Caddo. Throughout the region, the staple crops were generally the same—beans, corn, and squash. The farmers certainly did their share of hunting and fishing, but only to supplement food they raised from the earth. Their fields, or more precisely the rich soil itself, served as the hub around which daily and seasonal life revolved.

Over the plains, often far closer than the farmers would have liked, the nomadic and semi-nomadic hunters roamed, following the buffalo herds upon which they depended for survival. Their itinerant lifestyle set them in stark contrast to the agriculturists. Cherishing and defending unfettered access to the expansive grasslands, the buffalo hunters regularly came into conflict with villagers who lived more fixed lives. The arrival of the horse, courtesy of the Spanish conquistadors in the seventeenth and eighteenth centuries, only made matters worse; the hunters developed lifestyles that demanded even more space and encouraged greater mobility. Having almost totally abandoned the soil, tribes such as the Sioux, Cheyenne, Kiowa, and Pawnee routinely bullied sedentary farmers into supporting them with food, extorting crops from villagers through the threat of violence.

Not surprisingly, the social product of all this divergence and difference was a set of boundaries that clearly delineated the cultures of the Louisiana Territory. Even among the hunting tribes, competition for game led to the notion of "our" hunting ground

The Indians, nomadic and seminomadic hunters, tracked buffalo herds across miles of plains. These wanderers, from Sioux, Cheyenne, Kiowa, and Pawnee tribes, upset agricultural villages along the way, extorting food from farmers when hunting was lean. The hunt required access to many square miles of land, especially when the hunters traveled by horseback.

as opposed to "yours." Small-scale wars were common among the prairie nomads and mountain hunters who relied on animals other than the buffalo. Regardless of the exact location or target species, Native Americans defended their hunting grounds fiercely, and everyone knew which was whose.

When it came to the farmers, author Ted Morgan has argued that agriculture put people "in a different relationship with nature, because they are working the land instead of taking what it naturally offers." He concluded that "the farmer's attitude is territorial; the piece of land he works becomes *his* field, the crop *his* crop, grown with the sweat of *his* brow." The farmer, consequently, assumed "a defense role, as land disputes arise and marauders raid planted fields."[25] Like their hunting counterparts, then, the Native Americans who farmed land outside settled villages were locked into natural relationships that required them to erect and defend borders that defined a way of life as much as physical space. As noted in the *Encyclopedia of North American Indians*: "Populous tribes that engaged in big-game hunting, agriculture, or even large-scale seasonal gathering developed highly organized war complexes to defend their territorial boundaries." Notwithstanding the absence of what would be recognized as borders today, lines on maps delineating essentially political relationships, Native America was just as clearly demarcated by people who "viewed possession of land in a unique way. Tribes had well-defined, sacred territorial boundaries that literally defined who they were."[26]

Native Americans constructed various working relationships with and discrete mental images of nature. Despite a shared reverence for the land, disparate agendas and interests emerged. Boundaries, however flexible and fluid, materialized, separating societies and cultures. Farming folk knew where their parcels of land ended and those of neighboring groups began. Hunting tribes clearly staked out the bounds of areas from which they were currently taking game. Farmers and hunters alike recognized each other's legitimate claims to space. Those who worked the land set themselves apart from those who rode over it and vice versa. "Tribes recognized territorial boundaries," Gary Nash has written, even if they had no concept of private property rights.[27]

As this process of differentiation unfolded, distinct language groups began to emerge that pushed Native Americans further apart and reinforced their concept of cultural boundaries marking out locally unique ways of life. Communication, in short, became another border—nothing separates people more literally than the inability to understand what others are saying.

Languages varied tremendously over the area that would become the Louisiana Territory. Sioux speakers predominated on the rolling grasslands that stretched from the Dakotas into Oklahoma. Algonquin and Caddoan could be heard along the western edge of the region, an area roughly corresponding to the Rocky Mountains. Farther south into present-day Arkansas and the state of Louisiana, Native Americans spoke in the Muskegon tongue common to the American Southeast. Within these general divisions, specific dialects evolved that created local borders that often proved to be far less permeable than even their larger

NATIVE AMERICANS AND THE ENVIRONMENT

Indians, by necessity, lived with the natural world in a web of complex, interactive relationships. Material, concrete connections linked Native Americans to the land upon which their survival depended. Nature and the indigenous peoples were inextricably bound together. This fact implies that native peoples always and everywhere acted as good stewards of their environment. Recently, the romantic notion of the Indian as benevolent guardian of the ecosystem, maintaining, through some peculiar, mysterious wisdom, a "balance of nature," has been forcefully and convincingly challenged. The challenge, moreover, is directed toward those who credit Native Americans exclusively with profound concern for the natural world and perceive Europeans as being incapable of living in that world without destroying it through greed and a callous disregard for wild places and things. Probably the foremost critic of the "Indians-as-better-stewards" stereotype is Shepard Krech III.

Krech contends that Native American lifestyles were, in many cases, exploitative and ecologically damaging. Indians feared nature and knew their survival depended upon it but did not necessarily respect the environment. Their vision, in a sense, was wholly pragmatic. Krech argues that Native Americans never put nature before their own interests. He holds up as evidence not only rampant deforestation but also Native American commercial hunting that decimated the buffalo herds and beaver stocks long before Europeans ventured into the Louisiana Territory. In short, the myth of the ecological Indian, in Krech's opinion, "distorts culture. It masks cultural diversity ... because it has entered the realm of common sense and as received wisdom is perceived as a fundamental truth, it serves to deflect any desire to fathom or confront the evidence for relationships between Indians and the environment."[*] The only fair response to such weighty charges is that the early Native Americans acted just like what they were—people.

[*] Shepard Krech III, *The Ecological Indian: Myth and History.* New York: W.W. Norton, 1999, p. 27.

counterparts within which they were embedded. Taken together, the barriers put up by language became so great that some observers have concluded that "very few Indian tribes were able to communicate with their immediate neighbors."[28]

Native American languages and ways of life drew the first borders within the confines of the Louisiana Territory. These lines were fluid, often uncertain, boundaries, but they represented real, concrete interactions between human beings and the land they claimed as theirs. Native American borders circumscribed material relationships involving people who conceived of their world as a closed support system. In turn, these people imagined and built lifeways predicated upon organic connections with the prairies, rivers, and mountains. The physical place that came to be called the Louisiana Territory lived with the original inhabitants, and its rhythms were reflected in the fluidity of Native American borders.

This agreement between place and people was a far cry from the European model that supplanted it. The latter divorced itself entirely from the natural world in favor of its political cousin. The Europeans who began arriving in the 1500s came from homelands locked in seemingly endless political struggles that never failed to end in war. Bellicose, arrogant, and supremely suspicious, the conquerors developed an understanding and an imagery of the New World steeped in the dark waters of imperial intrigue and fear. What had been a natural space supporting an intimately interactive if not always peaceful human population, became a political rampart, walling off from each other aggressive and scheming European powers. Infused with life and no longer characterized by fluid internal borders, the Louisiana Territory became a political pawn.

4

Empires in
Louisiana

Spain came to the New World for gold and silver. The armies of conquistadors that began arriving in the early sixteenth century came to plunder the wealth of the great native empires of Central and South America—the Aztecs in Mexico and the Inca in Peru—and plunder they did. The Spanish methodically ransacked both empires, stripping them of the treasure Europeans craved so desperately at the time. Spanish soldiers, and the diseases that they carried, decimated the New World's human population, destroyed the indigenous societies, and mauled the native cultures. As early as 1542, the priest and advocate for Native American rights, Bartolome de Las Casas, lamented the fact that large swaths of the Americas were being transformed into "a wilderness" by the "inhumane and abominable villainies of the Spaniards." Las Casas protested that the lust for wealth had produced a bloodbath in which "twelve million souls innocently perished." The grieving priest then corrected himself: "I truly believe that I should be speaking within the truth if I were to say that over fifteen millions were consumed in this massacre."[29]

For many Spaniards, precious metals justified such vicious depredations. Slaughter and torture on a monumental scale were tolerated, with very few exceptions, because they made it possible to reap unheard-of profits. The Spanish drained from America 181 tons of gold and 16,000 tons of silver between the years 1500 and 1650 for one simple reason. In early modern Europe, as J.H. Elliot has observed, "Gold was power."[30] The Spanish became obsessed with the glittering metals they found. For them, America represented nothing less than a huge treasure trove to be systematically and thoroughly emptied. Little else seemed to matter. "Those lands [America]," wrote one bedazzled Spaniard in the 1520s, "do not produce bread or wine, but they do produce large quantities of gold, in which lordship consists."[31] The New World, according to the Spanish plan, was to be squeezed dry without mercy. Once Mexico had been totally looted, the seemingly empty expanses to the north were targeted.

The Spanish explorer Francisco Vasquez de Coronado, searching the American plains in vain for the fabled North American "city of gold" (1540–1542). Coronado pushed as far north as Kansas, finally turning back, empty handed. News of Coronado's failed exploits reached other Spanish explorers, and none bothered to retrace Coronado's footsteps, making him the last of the Spanish explorers to travel into what later became the United States of America.

For all their repulsive bloodletting, the early Spanish conquistadors developed, however briefly, a relationship with the land that resembled a twisted and tragic parody of the one crafted by the Native Americans. The Spanish crossed the Atlantic in order to draw out the precious ores that coursed through the mountains of the Americas, thus exhibiting a dependence on nature that, although greedily extractive, was quite real. Had the borders subsequently drawn by Europeans been founded on this connection alone, they would have been as concrete, in a strange sense, as those of the Indians. Spain, however, and France and England after it, was destined to drift in a different direction as the gold and silver stocks dwindled and imperial political concerns overrode raw avarice.

Fantasies of gold and silver lying about for the taking without a doubt animated early Spanish explorers and conquerors—fantasies that spun out tales of veritable cities of gold located somewhere in the center of North America. No one knew for certain where these golden cities were, but the vast plains west of the Mississippi River seemed a good bet. Rumors spread temptingly through Mexico of gold waiting for anyone bold enough to grab it. One Spaniard determined to test the cities-of-gold hypothesis was Francisco Vásquez de Coronado. Departing from Mexico in 1540, Coronado spent the next two years searching in vain for the rumored kingdom of gold. Although ultimately unsuccessful, the intrepid Coronado proved quite ambitious in his fruitless hunt. He and his party trudged as far north as modern-day Kansas before turning back disappointed and empty-handed. News of his failure ended the dreams of golden cities and cooled Spanish interest in the continental heartland. No Spanish explorer bothered to retrace Coronado's steps—that is, in search of gold.

Coronado might not have reached his shining goal, but his journey pushed the boundaries of Spanish influence and interest in North America to the point at which it came into contact with the leading edge of a similar probing by France. Explorers such as Jacques Cartier and Samuel de Champlain had been busily establishing a solid French presence in eastern Canada and the Great Lakes region since 1534. Their efforts paid handsome dividends in terms of imperial power, but it was the exertions of missionary Jacques Marquette and explorer Robert Cavelier, Sieur de La Salle, that put French outposts along the Mississippi River from modern-day Wisconsin to the Gulf of Mexico. Their expeditions opened the Louisiana Territory to permanent settlement and initiated the transition from Native American cultural to European political border arrangements.

Jacques Marquette took the leading role in the unfolding imperial drama in North America. Joining with a French adventurer named Louis Joliet, Marquette set out from Lake Michigan in May 1673 to explore the lands that lay to the west of the French settlement line. Following the river system, Marquette eventually entered the Mississippi near present-day

Prairie du Chien, Wisconsin. From there, the expedition floated down what the Indians called the Big River as far as what is now Arkansas, introducing the Native Americans to the new French overlords along the way. Soon after reaching the Arkansas River, however, Marquette died of dysentery, leaving the job of placing the Louisiana Territory firmly under the French flag to Sieur de La Salle.

La Salle began his trip southward along the Mississippi in late 1681. His route took his men through some of the most beautiful and dangerous parts of the continent. Finally, in April 1682, La Salle's company reached the mouth of the river. As the men and their leader gazed out over the Gulf of Mexico, they raised a rousing hurrah, fired their guns, and joined La Salle in claiming the Mississippi and all of the adjoining country in the name of the French king, Louis XIV. After thanking God, La Salle planted the French flag in the ground; the "fleur de lis" floated in the breeze over Louisiana. In an example of the carefree ingratitude Louis XIV was famous for, the king dismissed La Salle's accomplishment, calling Louisiana "quite useless."[32]

Just as the Spain was doing farther to the west, France began founding colonial settlements in what one writer termed "a vast domain [it] couldn't possibly manage."[33] At the time, management was a far less urgent concern than economic exploitation and the maintenance of a continuing presence in the face of Spanish expansion. What really mattered at this point, for both Spain and France, was a clear and undisputed identification of imperial spheres of influence. Neither kingdom seriously thought of the Louisiana country as an extension of its respective North American establishments; rather it was envisaged as a mutually acceptable buffer zone. The area from the Mississippi to the Rockies, in other words, was thought of as a unitary boundary that reassured each empire of its possessions. Certain and unassailable borders served the crucial purpose of making sure that two suspicious global competitors knew what territory belonged to whom and where. The place itself was almost an afterthought; politics was the thing.

By 1690, Spanish missions, forts known as *presidios*, and villages had sprung up in what would later become Texas and New Mexico. Spanish culture, religion, and language began to spread outward toward the deserts of the Southwest and the crashing waves of the Pacific Coast. Meanwhile, French forts and trading posts rose along the banks of the Mississippi and Missouri rivers, followed by towns large and small. All the while, the vast openness of the Louisiana Territory lay between the two European antagonists—shared but comfortingly divisive space, a true political border in every way.

SPANISH LOUISIANA

Spain never truly knew what to do with the Louisiana that Louis XV gave to his "dear and beloved cousin, the King of Spain" in 1762.* The territory's borders were hopelessly ill defined in its northern reaches, and little if any development had taken place except in the immediate vicinity of major rivers. The European population was tiny, perhaps only 13,000 people, and most of those were concentrated in the area in and around New Orleans. To make matters worse, the Spanish colonial administration proved as clumsy as it was corrupt, so much so that in 1768, after just six years of Spanish rule, the citizens of New Orleans petitioned France to "take back the colony instantly." The first Spanish governor was a brute; his successors were alternately lazy and greedy. As foreigners governing an alien population, most of the men Spain sent to North America concentrated on keeping the peace with Britain, and later the United States, and enriching themselves and their families. The territory seemed useless to royal officials in Spain, and the low quality of the administrators serving in Louisiana guaranteed that its growth would be stunted at best. According to one historian of French America, Louisiana under Spanish rule "was corruptly managed in every department [and] remained a considerable expense to Spain as it had been to France."** The Louisiana Purchase must have come as quite a relief to many in Europe and North America.

* Reuben Gold Thwaites, *France in America, 1497–1763*. New York: Harper & Brothers Publishers, 1905; reprint, Westport, Connecticut: Greenwood Press, Publishers, 1970, p. 281.

** Ibid., p. 294.

Both Spain and France moved aggressively to stake their claims in the continental center of North America. Neither saw much intrinsic value in the grassy steppes, snowy mountains, and lazy rivers that lay between them. They had even less respect for the indigenous inhabitants, unless of course the Native Americans could contribute to the imperial coffers of European monarchs. To be sure, access to the Mississippi River would become a hotly contested issue, directly involving both the Spanish and French crowns. Similarly, the fur and hide trade would become a staple of the French imperial economy, making settlers quite sensitive to incursions by Spanish merchants. For the time being, however, without any apparent resources such as gold and silver and sorely lacking in readily available arable land, Louisiana was given little thought by either France or Spain. The empires most certainly never conceived of the place as expressing some deeply-felt French or Spanish sense of collective self and purpose. Nor did either empire ever view it as some sort of vast stage upon which to act out a drama of divine mission, concepts that later became hallmarks of the United States phase of the Louisiana Territory's history.

For Spain and France, the principal value of Louisiana lay in its function as a frontier border, an edge of empire marking out distinct sets of interests and agendas. This function was highlighted as the English joined the colonial game ever more actively in the late seventeenth and early eighteenth centuries. In fact, by the 1700s, a three-way shoving match developed among the westward-leaning English colonies on the Atlantic coast, the French outposts on the Mississippi, and the Spanish settlements in the Southwest.

The intensity of the regional competition grew until war erupted. A great deal was at stake, particularly continental hegemony. It became obvious that whoever controlled the Louisiana Territory politically would sooner or later determine the fate of North America. Playing for such a prize, the imperial powers began drawing their borders more boldly and defending them with renewed vigor. The Europeans loved their maps and had always drawn lines to carve up the land those maps depicted. Now they began fighting over both the lines and the land.

Seven years after Sieur de La Salle named and claimed Louisiana for France, war broke out in Europe. For decades, the European monarchies had been jockeying for position in an ever-more crowded international marketplace. Trade, especially in the Atlantic sector with its profitable links between the Old World and the New, had become competitive to the point of armed conflict. The French, Spanish, English, and Dutch pursued hostile trade policies with obsessive ferocity. Thrown into this bitter mix were the antagonisms that clung to dynastic politics. By the late seventeenth century, Europe was primed for war.

The tensions finally broke in 1689. Known in Europe as the War of the League of Augsburg, King William's War became the first in a series of American wars of empire. Lasting until 1697, the conflict marked the start of a near century-long, titanic struggle in which Great Britain, Spain, and France vied for nothing less than total control over North America. During this time, Louisiana would slowly but surely move to the center of European political thinking regarding the alignment and allotment of power.

Its political value notwithstanding, Louisiana remained a backwater, barely settled for most of its yawning distance and occupied mostly by rough trappers, shrewd but often unscrupulous merchants, and almost ungovernable colonists. The overall condition and composition of Louisiana proved to be so wretched, in fact, that the French governor reported to the crown in 1710 that the "people are a heap of the dregs of Canada" and that the entire territory was "not worth a straw at the present time."[34] Nonetheless, merely eight years after the governor's gloomy report, France moved "to complete its military 'encirclement' of the English colonies" and reinforce its border with Spain by founding the settlement of New Orleans to anchor the remainder of Louisiana.[35]

After the initial engagement in the 1690s, England, France,

and Spain fought each other, in various allied configurations, twice more before the final rupture in North American imperial relations took place in 1754. Beginning rather inadvertently as a minor skirmish in the forests near what became Pittsburgh, Pennsylvania, the French and Indian War (called "the Seven Years' War" in Europe) raged for nine blood-soaked years, pitting the British and their American colonists against the French and Spanish. When the shooting finally stopped and the peace negotiations began in Paris in 1763, Louisiana loomed large on the table.

Britain sensed its command of the moment. All of the parties understood that after sweeping victories on land and sea, the peace was Britain's to make. It would surely snatch Canada and key Caribbean islands from France; the English king's representatives would just as certainly demand unchallenged dominion over India where the French had been making significant commercial inroads. The Spanish accepted the fact that the British would try to wrest Florida from them. The only real question mark, in fact, involved the fate of Louisiana. The empire that controlled it would likely control the future of North America.

The French correctly surmised that if they lost Louisiana, in addition to Canada, to their mortal enemies, the British, they might as well abandon all hope of further influence anywhere on the continent. Any lingering possibility of regaining their former position would be snuffed out. British control of the Mississippi and the port of New Orleans would open the entire region from the Appalachians westward to American farmers whose produce would flow down the great river just as steadily as the profits from its sale would flow to British merchants. The British would never relinquish such a commercial godsend. Once ceded, the Louisiana Territory would be gone for good.

The French, therefore, concluded that a transfer of Louisiana to the British had to be avoided above all else. A conspiracy took shape with the aim of shifting possession of Louisiana to the Spanish before the British could demand it for themselves. A more or less reliable French ally, Spain was devoutly Catholic (like France), rigidly monarchist (again, like France), and suffused with an abiding hatred for everything English. The Spanish, so French thinking went, might hold onto Louisiana as caretakers until some unspecified point in the future. When the time was right, France could reassert sovereignty and reestablish the *status quo ante* in North America. The French hoped someday to turn back time and continue their imperial rule as if the wartime defeat of the 1760s had never taken place. This was a foolish hope to be sure, but Britain, from the French perspective, simply could not be allowed to take, hold, and exploit Louisiana.

To this end, the French devised a cunning plan simultaneously to lose *and* keep Louisiana. France offered to give the territory to Spain as something of a gift. Claiming for public consumption that Louisiana had cost the king's treasury "eight hundred thousand livres a year, without yielding a sou in return," France proposed to hand the place over to Spain before negotiating with Britain.[36]

Spain was unnerved and even somewhat insulted by the proposition. No one in Spain really wanted a huge chunk of American real estate that the Spanish could not govern, afford, or do anything productive with. Nevertheless, the Spanish crown, which had no good reason to accept France's self-serving largesse, accepted the offer for its own reasons. Spain had no desire to see the British in control of the Mississippi and did not relish the notion of British colonists and traders prowling the borders of Spanish Mexico. These factors alone made Spain envision nothing but smuggling, territorial disputes, and perhaps even invasion. Clearly the only way to avert these hypothetical threats and maintain Spanish power was to accept, albeit grudgingly, the French "gift." In late 1762, Louisiana became, at least for the time being, part of Spanish America.

With Louisiana safely in the care of its Iberian ally, France sat down to hammer out the details of a peace treaty with Britain, which, as was its due, received the choice fruits of victory. Canada, Florida, India, and the best of France's Caribbean islands all went to the British. The western lands between the

Appalachian Mountains and the Mississippi, including the much-coveted Ohio country, similarly changed hands. This particular concession gave Britain a "natural" border at the Mississippi River, in essence splitting North America into two halves—one British and one Spanish—between Canada and Mexico. France was no longer a factor; its continental position had evaporated.

Curiously, Britain never pressed either France or Spain on the issue of Louisiana. The likely reason is that, much like Spain, Britain saw no compelling reason to ask for land for which it had no use. The Indian trade, river highways, and arable land that the crown and the American colonies desired so deeply lay to the east of the Mississippi. As long as the great muddy river itself remained open to New Orleans-bound traffic, there seemed to be no point in arguing over an empty, grass-covered wasteland. Britain was content to let the Spanish and the "savage" Indians have it.

When it came to the Louisiana Territory, France lost what it had, Spain got what it did not want, and Britain let the matter slide. Louisiana in 1763, moreover, began to lose its primary function as an imperial border. With France gone, Spain and Britain faced one another uneasily but quietly. The political landscape, however, had been irrevocably altered. Both empires acknowledged the Mississippi as the dividing line between their American possessions, but Britain established a far more important internal border along the spine of the Appalachian Mountains. In a bid to take the place of the French as economic partner among the western Indians with as little disruption as possible, the British partitioned their lands between the Indians and the colonists, now both under British authority. Britain established a boundary at the Appalachians, the Proclamation Line of 1763, and put in place a system for regulating relations across it. Most significantly, the royal government ordered American settlers to respect the line and forbade trespassing under any circumstances.

The war with France had cost Britain dearly. The government

in London wanted nothing more than peace in North America, knowing it could ill-afford to keep defending the colonies against Indian attacks such as those that occurred during Pontiac's Rebellion in 1763. A nice, bold map line backed up by a string of frontier forts seemed like the answer to Britain's problem. It was not a lucrative or even popular solution. British Indian agents and fur traders never succeeded in replicating among the western tribes the reputation for fairness that the French had enjoyed. Worse yet, colonial farmers and politicians fumed at the idea of being denied millions of fertile acres, not to mention access to the Mississippi, all because some administrator 3,000 miles away in London chose to cater to Indian needs over theirs. What appeared to royal eyes as simply one more imperial boundary became an incendiary issue capable of lighting the fuse of revolution, a revolution that would bring new eyes and a new agenda to Louisiana. Culture and politics would soon be subordinated to ideology as the Louisiana Territory's borders began to metamorphose yet again.

5

A New
Neighbor

The American Revolution dramatically altered the balance of power in North America. A brand-new player arrived on the scene, a player infused with overwhelming ambition and exuding supreme confidence and energy. Great Britain, an established imperial force, had sought stability, order, peace, and profit during its brief period of dominance after the French and Indian War. After the revolution, it was replaced by an aggressive young republic that was determined to expand its borders and influence. From the very beginning, the new United States of America charted a course toward geopolitical supremacy. The fledgling country set itself the task of spreading its culture, specifically its national ideology, over the entire continent.

Americans, in appreciable numbers, began drifting across the Appalachians toward the Mississippi as early as the 1760s and 1770s. Most were looking for nothing more than a piece of arable land to farm, land that would be gained at the expense of Native Americans. The Proclamation Line of 1763 had to be violated in practice and principle in order to do so, but this imperial contrivance was roundly hated and generally ignored by frontier farmers anyway. The line fenced them in, so these people felt, and kept them from claiming and utilizing land that the current owners had left criminally fallow. Frontier settlers saw no point in allowing prime tracts to sit idle while Indians greedily traded furs and, by their mere presence, helped Britain keep the peace with Spain. Great Britain, colonists argued, had drawn the Proclamation Line in order to reconfigure imperial borders in its own interests. Even before the Revolutionary War began, Americans had set their sights on new lands and new interpretations of what that land meant. Now they were determined to make the land theirs. The Louisiana Territory's imperial-political phase was about to end.

After years of legislative wrangling and disputes between Great Britain and its grumbling American colonies, matters finally turned to arms in 1775. War broke out within one of the three great empires rather than among them. Initially, the British, with their superior military might, gained the upper hand, but as the war dragged on, American victories slowly mounted. The entry of France and Spain on the American side tilted the balance even further. Here and there, people began to consider seriously the possibility of British failure and colonial independence. The territory of an independent American state, everyone agreed, would likely include the area adjoining the Ohio River and the trans-Appalachian West. A Mississippi River border for the new nation would necessarily follow, putting it into direct contact with the Spanish Empire. One of the world's youngest countries would stand face to face with one of the oldest along the eastern edge of Louisiana. The indirect alliance with the Spanish, through the French, did little to ease the anxiety of those who predicted trouble in the future.

Devastating defeats at Saratoga (1777) and Yorktown (1781) convinced the British king and parliament that the American war was a failed cause. Two more fruitless years of combat proved it beyond any doubt. In September 1783, British and American representatives signed a peace treaty in Paris. With their signatures, these men brought into the world a sovereign union of former colonies, the United States. It is important to understand that this was no mere assemblage of former provinces suddenly on their own. This was a country that believed itself to be ordained by God and by divine destiny. Americans long conceived of themselves as being blessed with "the spiritual and physical resources to become a self-reliant, mighty New World 'empire.'"[37] More to the point, the United States "used the word empire in the sense of a country embracing an extended area," in this case, the totality of North America.[38]

As a document, the Paris treaty first and foremost acknowledged American independence, but in the process, it established the western boundary of the nation at the Mississippi River. According to the treaty, the new border ran "along the middle of the said river Mississippi," but only to "the thirty-first degree of north latitude." From there it cut "due east ... [to] the river Apalachicola."[39] Considering that the Spanish still retained

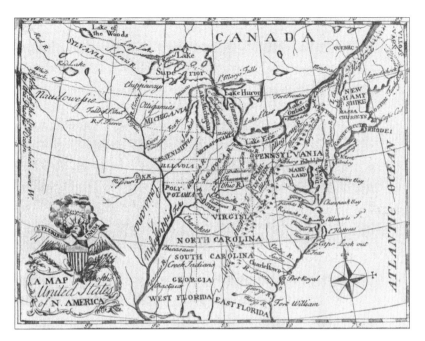

A map of the eastern seaboard of the United States, with details spanning northern Florida to New Hampshire and to just west of the Mississippi, 1784. Farmers and others began settling the fertile Mississippi River basin as early as the 1760s and 1770s, disregarding the British-drawn Proclamation Line of 1763. They chose, instead, to brave the frontier to explore a new land, to better themselves and their families.

effective possession of Louisiana and had reacquired Florida, the rather vaguely drawn Mississippi border almost immediately caused tensions to rise, especially in the area between Georgia and the great river. Here, both Spain and the United States claimed ownership: the latter citing the treaty with Britain and the former maintaining that the real boundary lay further north. The Spanish said that the territory was part of Florida and argued for a physical connection between Florida and Louisiana far above New Orleans; the Americans saw the old Southwest as rightfully theirs if, as they presumed, the new border ran logically straight down the middle of the Mississippi. The core of the problem was that the Spanish refused to accept any definition of a Mississippi boundary other than one that gave them total control over the river for most of its southern length. The underlying motive for all of this wrangling was that the river had served as the political boundary of Spanish interests and influence in North America since 1762, and Spain intended to keep it that way.

From Spain's perspective, Louisiana functioned nicely as a buffer between empires, and it should continue to do so in its most recent incarnation as an international boundary zone. Control of the Mississippi was crucial in this respect. Whether or not Spain actually intended to settle and develop Louisiana was beside the point. As far as the Spanish were concerned, Louisiana, and its southern extension through the disputed territory to Florida, operated as a vital check on American expansion and pretensions. Spain, in other words, persisted in thinking politically when it came to Louisiana; the kingdom still saw the place in an outdated imperial light. The Spanish never anticipated that the upstart Americans might see it differently.

The Spanish, in the end, were blind to the fact that the world had changed; the old imperial system was dying. For this reason, Spain turned out to be utterly unprepared for the disputes that arose within just a few months of American independence. Nor was the Spanish crown ready for the dogged determination exhibited by the United States in pursuit of its territorial demands and ideological goals. The Spanish simply lacked the foresight to anticipate how important access to the Mississippi and the port of New Orleans would be to their eager and aggressive young neighbor. They would soon find out.

Despite critical assistance given to the Americans, at great expense to the treasury of Louis XVI, France gained nothing in 1783. The British held on to Canada, and Spain held on to Louisiana. Revolutionary stirrings at home soon distracted the French. For Spain it was a very different story. As the British pulled out of their former colonies and opened the trans-Appalachian lands to settlement, Louisiana's borders came alive with activity. American farmers, merchants, traders, and entrepreneurs of every type spilled over the mountains toward the Mississippi. The sight of so many Americans moving in their direction unnerved the Spanish. The fact that these people came carrying an ideology that justified expansion in religious terms did not add any comfort. The sentiments expressed by Ezra Stiles in his essay "The United States Elevated to Glory and Honour," which was published in 1783, were typical. Stiles wrote of an American citizenry that would "become a great people," dwelling in "a great, a very great nation" charged by heaven to "illumine the world with TRUTH and LIBERTY." He continued:

> Already does the new constellation of the United States begin to realize this glory: And we have reason to hope, and I believe to expect, that God has still greater blessings in store for this vine which his own right hand hath planted, to make us 'high among the nations in praise, and in name, and in honour.'[40]

Such assumptions of moral purpose and clear declarations of expansive intent prompted the Spanish to amplify their calls for sovereignty over the disputed territory lying east of New Orleans. What was even more troubling was that that Spain openly challenged the American claim to free navigation of the Mississippi and the right to deposit goods at New Orleans, a curious challenge given Spain's rather weak strategic position. Technically, of course, Spain could limit river traffic and close New Orleans if it wanted, especially considering the uncertainty of the post-Revolution border, but the kingdom was in no position to enforce such restrictions. It had no credible military force to speak of in Louisiana or Florida, at least not one capable of waging even a limited war against the Americans. Furthermore, the empire in general was bankrupt and crumbling; by the end of the eighteenth century, the Spanish monarchy was on the verge of collapse. For all its anxious bluster, Spain had neither the resources nor the muscle to defend Louisiana, let alone project imperial power indefinitely. This fact did not stop it from trying.

U.S. Foreign Affairs Secretary John Jay (1745–1829). In one of his first diplomatic forays, in 1786, Jay met with Spanish ambassador Diego de Gardqui to negotiate a deal to open the Mississippi River and the port of New Orleans to American ships and trade. The diplomats were unable to reach a mutually favorable agreement, however, and America looked for other ways to gain access to the areas in dispute.

In 1784, Louisiana's Spanish governor unilaterally closed the Mississippi to American shipping and revoked the right of deposit at New Orleans. The governor then began brazenly selling guns to the Indians, encouraging them to attack American frontier settlements. Authorities in New Orleans went so far as to try to bribe a disgruntled American general, James Wilkinson, into betraying his country by seizing and handing over to Spain the disputed Southwest. This ridiculous and clumsy attempt at international intrigue only made matters worse by turning a diplomatic dispute into an affair of national honor. Meanwhile, American farmers watched crops rot and goods go unsold for two years. The Louisiana Territory's eastern boundary seethed with anger and discontent.

Sensing rightly that something had to be done quickly, the United States moved to set things straight in 1786. In one of its first diplomatic forays, the United States sent its foreign affairs secretary, John Jay, to meet with Spain's ambassador, Diego de Gardoqui. The men knew and respected each other, but no agreement on the pressing issues of the day could be reached. The United States firmly demanded free access to the Mississippi along its entire length and an unassailable right of deposit at New Orleans. Spain, for its part, asserted the privileges of ownership and rejected American demands. The Spanish had never really wanted either the Mississippi or New Orleans; both simply came as part of the Louisiana package foisted on them by the French. In the charged political atmosphere of the time, however, Spain was loath to compromise its power over either. Louisiana might not have been much, but to the decrepit Spanish monarchy, it represented the empire's best defense against a precocious United States.

After some maneuvering, Gardoqui convinced Jay to accept a horrible deal. The United States would give up any and all navigation claims on the Mississippi for 25 years and confirm all Spanish possessions in the Western Hemisphere, including Louisiana. In return, Spain would sign a trade treaty and, of all things, promise to defend the borders of the United States. No one asked by what means.

Needless to say, the Americans rejected the agreement. The trade treaty appeared to favor New England merchants exclusively; conceding the closure of the Mississippi promised to cripple Western farmers. Worst of all, validating Spain's possessions abruptly dowsed the fiery ideological aspirations of Americans who envisaged expansion as a divine right. Spanish Louisiana stood like a grassy wall between the United States and the rest of the continent to the Pacific, a vast remnant of a bygone era of European hegemony. Guaranteeing Spanish holdings threatened to stunt the growth of the young republic, and this was simply unthinkable. The negotiations ended with the Mississippi still closed, New Orleans docks still cleared of American goods, and Louisiana still solidly Spanish.

The years between 1786 and 1795 saw changes taking place both within and beyond the United States. A constitution that stabilized the political situation in the country and increased the authority and efficiency of the federal government was finally ratified in 1788. The American economy improved, thanks to the efforts of Alexander Hamilton, the first secretary of the treasury. Under President George Washington's leadership, a trade and territorial treaty with Great Britain was hammered out. Jay's Treaty, as it was called, cleared up lingering doubts about the Canadian border and required the British to evacuate forts that it continued to occupy on American soil. Washington himself saw to it that the treaty was pushed through the Senate just before a similar effort began with Spain regarding the Mississippi and New Orleans.

Talks with Spain stalled after the Jay-Gardoqui debacle. For almost ten years, Spain and the United States glared at one another across the great muddy river that divided them. At last, in 1795, another American mission, this one led by veteran politician Thomas Pinckney, went to Spain to negotiate an end to the impasse. Pinckney, against all expectations, succeeded in record time. The Spanish, it turned out, had more important things on their minds than their dreary backwater possession in North America and the petty disputes its administration caused with the United States. A revolution had broken out in France that had resulted in the execution of King Louis XVI. Events in France soon threatened to engulf all of Europe in a wave of republican violence and war. Spain had already been drawn into a military coalition against the French revolutionary regime and now worried about the possibility, however remote, of defeat. The Spanish king, fearful for his own realm and life, fixed his attention and that of his government on affairs closer to home, making Pinckney's job all the easier.

With such well-prepared diplomatic ground, Pinckney scored a major and much-needed victory at the bargaining table, and the Treaty of San Lorenzo was signed in 1795. In its articles, the negotiators spelled out American rights, including free access to the Mississippi, the unrestricted right of deposit at New Orleans, and a 31°N border with Florida that gave all of the disputed old Southwest to the United States. According to the treaty, "the western boundary of the United States which separates them from the Spanish colony of Louisiana" continued to run "in the middle of the channel or bed of the River Mississippi." It was further agreed that "the navigation of said river, in its whole breadth from its source to the ocean," was open to Americans without exception.[41]

Spain, in fact, gave the United States everything it wanted in return for some minor trade concessions and a pledge from its neighbor to work to prevent Indian raids originating on its side of the border. Now the United States could claim unalloyed possession of everything from Canada to Florida and from the Atlantic to the Mississippi. Unintentionally, however, the Treaty of San Lorenzo also pointed the United States directly toward Louisiana.

Just as the ink dried on Pinckney's Treaty, the French Revolution imploded. The excesses of the Reign of Terror, in which hundreds of innocent people lost their lives under the blade of the guillotine, provoked a conservative backlash. By the end of 1795, the radical National Convention had been replaced by the Directory, a more sedate and less bloody governing body, which discovered a savior for France in the person of a little Corsican general named Napoleon Bonaparte.

Napoleon, calculating and ruthless, soon parlayed a military victory in Italy and a well-camouflaged defeat in Egypt into political influence. When the Directory proved unable to provide France with the order and stability its citizens craved, a new administration, the Consulate, took charge. Napoleon moved quickly to gain a place as one of the consuls and almost immediately assumed dictatorial powers. Once his place was secure, Napoleon began plotting revenge against France's long-time enemy, the despised British, not only in Europe but around the world. He planned to regroup France's army and navy, launch a global offensive to crush the British once and for all, and dominate Europe. The diminutive dictator also harbored grandiose illusions concerning a new French empire in North America. Toward this end, he had to check the further expansion of the United States.

Louisiana was the key here. Napoleon figured that if he resumed control over the territory and reversed the transfer agreement of 1762, he could station a French garrison along the Mississippi and erect what his chief minister, Charles de Talleyrand, dubbed a "wall of brass" in the way of American westward movement. If he succeeded in doing so, Napoleon thought, France might be able to convince American farmers in the Mississippi valley, oriented as they were toward the river and New Orleans, to secede from the rest of the country and ally themselves with his reinvigorated empire. At the heart of this scheme, according to Robert Tucker and David Hendrickson, was the assumption that "Louisiana might serve alternately as a magnet and a barrier."[42] Napoleon hoped to gain a degree of coercive influence over North America that had been denied even to the greatest of French kings.

Sensing Napoleon's predatory intentions, Spain's King Charles IV made overtures toward his belligerent northern neighbor. These overtures culminated in the Treaty of Ildefonzo (1800). The treaty, a rather transparent effort to cozy up to a dangerous and unpredictable ally, secretly transferred Louisiana back to the French. It was a transfer that directly threatened the security and the territorial ambitions of the United States. Worse still, Napoleon's move undermined the ideological foundations upon which the Americans were constructing their nation and their collective identity. If the trans-Mississippi West were denied them, the project that many Americans believed God himself had been the architect of would come to a shuddering halt. Talleyrand's "wall of brass" might end forever the quasi-biblical American quest for continental dominion.

Spain, obviously feeling that everyone would find out soon enough anyway, revealed its secret agreement with France in October 1802. After making the transfer of Louisiana to France public and official, Spanish authorities promptly closed New Orleans to American shipping. In an instant, American diplomatic policy and national security were thrown into turmoil. Farmers and merchants feared the worst and demanded that the government do something. The American representative in New Orleans wrote to then-Secretary of State James Madison that the "difficulties and risks" to the national economy presented by the port's closure "are incalculable." President Jefferson himself stated flatly that there "is on the globe one single spot" that the United States simply had to possess and that was "New Orleans, through which the produce of three-eights of our territory must pass to market." The *New York Evening Post* fumed in an editorial that an American army should be sent to take New Orleans by force in order to safeguard "the future destiny of North America." Commenting on the importance of the Mississippi River valley to Westerners, Madison declared that the "Mississippi is to them everything, [it is] all the navigable rivers of the Atlantic States, formed into one stream."[43]

The American enterprise was in crisis. The promise of a universal republican order, or at least one that spanned the continent, many Americans lamented, had been compromised by the shadowy dealings of the most corrupt and decadent of the European monarchies, Bourbon Spain, and a resurgent French empire out to rule the world. What might happen next, no one hazarded to guess. The French menace would soon sit squarely in Louisiana. Jefferson, sitting in the new capital city of Washington, D.C., did not have the luxury of time; he had to act quickly and decisively. So he picked up his pen—and wrote.

6

Mr. Jefferson's Purchase

On April 18, 1802, the president put pen to paper and wrote a brief letter to the American representative in France, Robert R. Livingston. "The cession of Louisiana ... works most sorely on the United States," Jefferson began. Due to its "feeble state," Spain had never been a genuine threat, an irritant perhaps, but never a threat. Napoleon's France was another matter altogether: "the impetuosity of her temper, the energy and restlessness of her character, placed [her] in a point of eternal friction with us." Napoleon's aggressive pursuit of his imperial ends and the dictator's outright ambition made "it impossible that France and the United States can continue long friends." Jefferson continued, "The day that France takes possession of New Orleans fixes the sentence which is to restrain [the United States] forever within her low-water mark ... This is not a state of things we seek or desire." The only possible avenue open would be to buy New Orleans before Napoleon could consolidate his position there. Jefferson ordered Livingston to approach the French government on this point and propose a deal. The president concluded by reminding his emissary of the gravity of his assignment: "Every eye in the United States is now fixed on the affairs of Louisiana."[44]

By the early nineteenth century, Americans were renowned for their restless acquisitiveness. Confident and energetic, Americans believed themselves to be the sole legitimate font of republican values and democratic ideals. Always searching the horizon with effervescent optimism, they viewed most borders, especially the wholly political ones left over from the imperial period, as minor obstacles. The imperial powers hid behind their borders; Americans yearned to erase them. As journalist John Leland has written, "While Europeans sought to protect their boundaries, Americans saw their destiny in endless expansion."[45]

Compelled to draw new lines based on ideology rather than solely on politics or culture, Americans created new, abstract boundaries for their westward-driving republic. Although politics and culture were not entirely absent from the process, ideas were the engine. The core of these ideas revolved around the nation's providence-directed mission. Americans understood their project as much more than simply defining physical relationships or establishing defensive boundaries. American borders, constantly being scrutinized and adjusted, implied movement. Expansion, demographic and geographic, stood as a constant that united a proud and diverse people. An agenda of mobility and change typified nineteenth-century America. Nowhere would this become more obvious than in Louisiana.

Victory in the revolution against Great Britain had brought the United States to the banks of the Mississippi; years of diplomatic maneuvering had positioned the country to move westward. God himself seemed to be pointing out the direction toward which Americans should aim their ambitions and their wagons. Now, however, the American people imagined that an alien coalition of Spain and France conspired to resurrect an imperial barrier to further growth.

Spain's collusion in Napoleon's scheme to restore French power to North America demanded timely, bold action by the nation's president, Thomas Jefferson. By nature cautious in the use of his authority and always keen to limit the executive power of government, Jefferson had to move with uncharacteristic force. He knew well that the courts of Europe, including Napoleon's, respected sharp dealing and hard bargaining. The timid party in any negotiation soon found itself at a crippling disadvantage. European diplomats plied their trade aggressively and with consummate skill.

Forced into an ill-fitting proactive role, Jefferson labored to check the French. He proposed a deal to Napoleon: He would buy New Orleans and whatever surrounding lands France was willing to sell. Jefferson accurately guessed that since the French had as yet invested very little in terms of money and manpower in Louisiana, they might be persuaded to give it up. Dangling cash in front of Napoleon, in exchange for territory he as yet had little apparent use for, might gain what the United States sought. Ownership of New Orleans would protect American commerce, promote agricultural development, and ensure continued progress toward Jefferson's goal of seeding the continent with democratic ideals and institutions.

New Orleans and the Mississippi River had to be placed firmly under the guiding hand of the United States. The rest of Louisiana was something of a mystery to most Americans, including Jefferson. Writing to the Kentucky's Senator John Breckenridge, Jefferson admitted, "on the subject of Louisiana ... Our information as to the country is very incomplete."[46] Little was known about this wild expanse beyond the immediate area along the lower Mississippi, and few people gave the place much thought. Rumors abounded that Louisiana trembled under the feet of wooly mammoths and giant beavers; more incredible were stories of mountains of solid salt and of lost tribes of Indians who spoke Welsh. Despite the mystery, Jefferson wanted New Orleans. His decision to make an offer for it unintentionally set into motion the third and final phase of the Louisiana Territory's evolution, one that promised to usher in a new understanding of the function of arbitrary borders.

In Paris, Livingston went to work. He had been instructed to acquire New Orleans and western Florida if the opportunity presented itself. The French, however, curiously began making noises about a sale of the entire colony of Louisiana. Without clear authority to consider such a package, Livingston kept his focus on New Orleans. Luckily, the envoy was not destined to sit at the bargaining table alone. Sensing that Livingston, a timid and rather conservative man, might be facing a task beyond his abilities, Jefferson dispatched future president James Monroe to Paris in order to strengthen the American hand.

Monroe arrived in Europe ready to deal and authorized to spend up to $10 million if he had to. Monroe soon found out that more than money was needed to play in the European game. Napoleon's ministers, first among them Charles de Talleyrand, were experienced in the ways of manipulation and intimidation. They toyed mischievously with both Monroe and Livingston, seeing in them little besides provincial naïveté. As Napoleon himself told Livingston, "You have come to a very

James Monroe and Robert Livingston negotiate the Lousiana Purchase with French Minister Talleyrand, in Paris, 1803. The return of the land to the French by Spain in 1800 presented an opportunity for America to resolve the problem of the closure of the Mississippi River and the port of New Orleans to American ships and trade. Moreover, U.S. ownership of the land would encourage America's Manifest Destiny to expand its lands from ocean to ocean.

corrupt world."[47] Talleyrand and his compatriots purposely left the American pair dangling while they weighed their options. Napoleon had grand fantasies of dominating not only Europe but also the Americas. He rarely thought small. On this occasion, however, he had more than overweening ambition bearing down on him.

War, once again, seemed likely in Europe. In fact, Napoleon had already accepted the inevitability of a decisive clash with his old nemesis, Great Britain. He planned to strike first, yet the timing of any resumption of hostilities depended upon French finances and the outcome of a minor rebellion far across the Atlantic. An uprising against French rule had broken out on the island of Haiti. Led by a former slave and ex-French Army officer, Toussaint L'Ouverture, Haiti's blacks had rebelled, determined to shake off their French masters and declare independence. Napoleon acted on his first instinct and sent troops to the Caribbean to smash the rebels. Nature and his adversaries, however, had different plans. Yellow fever burned through the French force, while L'Ouverture's insurgents fought tenaciously. Instead of reasserting French authority, Napoleon was presented with the very real possibility of defeat. Haiti soured the French dictator on the notion of a new French empire in America. Tired of his Haitian troubles and needing cash badly to prepare for war against Great Britain, Napoleon suddenly felt very generous toward Livingston and Monroe.

Analyzing current events, Napoleon agreed, in early 1803, to sell New Orleans to the United States and to throw in the rest of Louisiana to round out the deal. This sudden turnaround shocked Napoleon's advisers. When his own brother protested, the French emperor responded, "Think what you please about it. I have decided to sell Louisiana to the Americans."[48] To his staff, Napoleon explained that despite knowing "the full value of Louisiana, [and being] desirous of repairing the fault of the French negotiator who abandoned it in 1763," he had made up his mind "to renounce Louisiana."

"It is not only New Orleans that I will cede," Napoleon declared, "it is the whole colony without reservation." He then noted almost as an aside that the acquisition of Louisiana "strengthens for ever the power of the United States."[49] The sale, for Napoleon, represented a purely political move in which he calculated precisely the costs and benefits. In this, he saw Louisiana one last time through imperial eyes. Concerning the territory's actual borders with Spanish America, Napoleon felt it best to leave them purposely vague. Reflecting on the fictional qualities of the imperial border system, Napoleon remarked that "If an obscurity did not always exist, it would be perhaps a good policy to put one there."[50] A nice little boundary dispute between the United States and Spain would keep both powers busy while France expanded and consolidated its position in Europe. More than that, it would make any kind of reconciliation between the United States and Great Britain less likely than it already was, considering Jefferson's suspicion of anything

British. All of this spelled out a single fact: Napoleon wanted the United States to take Louisiana off his hands permanently.

Monroe and Livingston accepted France's offer and put up a

SLAVERY AND THE LOUISIANA PURCHASE

Thomas Jefferson championed liberty and freedom and accepted, at least theoretically, the concept of equality. Jefferson, however, was a man of his time and was, to boot, a Southerner who owned slaves. For all of his talk about freedom and dignity, Jefferson was at best ambivalent toward the institution of slavery as it had developed in the late-eighteenth and early-nineteenth centuries. When it came to the slave system's expansion into the Louisiana Territory, Jefferson understood that Southern farmers and planters would certainly take their slaves with them into the new land, and he opposed this in principle. He was equally aware, however, that conflict would surely follow any attempt to prohibit slavery in Louisiana. Such a prohibition had been successfully applied to the old Northwest in 1787, but the Louisiana Territory, extending deeply into the South as it did, was another matter entirely.

The ideological-cultural clash that Jefferson anticipated was previewed in the debates that erupted in the Senate over slavery and Louisiana as the purchase agreement with France was being considered. Senators opposed to slavery's spread agreed with their colleague Samuel White who stated emphatically that there was "nothing in the treaty that guarantees to the people of that country the power, I will not say the right, of holding slaves." Jefferson's personal friend, Kentucky's Senator John Breckenridge, set his opposition in even starker terms: "The treaty does not in the smallest degree authorize that people to hold slaves ... I consider slavery as an evil—and am for confining it within as small a compass as possible."[*] Slavery's supporters responded with similar force. Georgia's James Jackson pleaded that "without the aid of slaves ... neither coffee nor cotton can be raised" in Louisiana, "slavery must be admitted into that territory." One of Jackson's fellow senators claimed that the Americans who would settle Louisiana "wish for African slaves ... we ought to let them have a supply."[**] Jefferson and the other politicians involved in the purchase debate died long before the issue was finally put to rest—on the battlefields of the Civil War.

* Roger G. Kennedy, *Mr. Jefferson's Lost Cause: Land, Farmers, Slavery, and the Louisiana Purchase.* New York: Oxford University Press, 2003, p. 211.

** Ibid., p. 211–212.

total of $15 million in combined cash and credits for the whole of Louisiana. When the purchase agreement arrived in Washington, Congress grumbled loudly. Questions were raised about the money and Jefferson's constitutional authority to enter into such a deal. The president himself acknowledged that he had "done an act beyond the Constitution," but argued that, like any good guardian, he had purchased "an important adjacent territory ... for your good."[51] Given the fact that the papers had already been signed and considering the discount price, a mere three cents per acre by modern calculations, the purchase was confirmed, and the United States took possession of the Louisiana Territory.

Now came the real work of determining just what the nation's $15 million had bought. President Jefferson needed to find out exactly what lay beyond the Mississippi. Maps would have to be drawn and scientific observations made. The president wanted the plants and animals catalogued and the lifeways of the indigenous peoples recorded. Only after seeing what the country had could the president decide what to make of it.

Jefferson's first move was to put together a team of men for an expedition through the heart of Louisiana; it would be called the Corps of Discovery. To lead this hardy—some said foolhardy— band, the president tapped his secretary, an army officer named Meriwether Lewis. Lewis's second in command would be an old friend from the service, William Clark.

Lewis was a vigorous, 29-year-old career soldier who had served with Clark on the frontier before the latter resigned in 1796. The men got along and worked well together. Lewis recalled Clark fondly even after being transferred to President Jefferson's personal staff. When Jefferson approached Lewis about commanding the Corps of Discovery, the young officer quickly floated Clark's name for consideration of a command. The president consented readily, seeing in the pair a good balance and a strong bond, and set the men to work.

Lewis and Clark put together a 50-man expedition that included soldiers and boatmen as well as Clark's personal slave, a man known simply as York, the only African American in the company. In order to collect supplies and acclimate themselves to the West, the Corps sequestered itself in a rudely constructed fort near St. Louis for the winter of 1803–1804. As soon as the weather permitted, the team set out for the Missouri River, its highway into the Louisiana Territory. Following the water upstream, the expedition penetrated deep into a place few non-Indians had ever seen. Lewis and Clark, as instructed, noted each and every new find or curiosity they came across.

Traveling by canoe for the first leg of their journey, the men described in their notebooks river currents strong enough to snap tow lines and drive boats ashore. Simultaneously, they marveled at how "rich & well timbered" the shoreline seemed to be.[52] Clark wrote excitedly that wherever their canoes took them, the riverbanks were crowded with life. On one stretch of water, he wrote that the shore "abounds in Dear Elk & Bear," complaining in the same breath that the "Ticks & Musquiters are verry troublesome."[53]

As the Corps of Discovery continued, they made frequent contact with Native Americans. These encounters were generally occasions for trade and mutual satisfaction of curiosity, but more than once, suspicion and anxiety nearly resulted in bloodshed. Clark, for example, noted one meeting in September 1804 during which a group of Sioux were invited aboard one of the boats. Hoping to create a positive atmosphere, Clark offered some whiskey to his guests. As the full effect of the drink set in, the men became belligerent. "Most of the Warriers appeared to have their Bows strung," Clark wrote, "and took out ther arrows from the quiver." Lewis and the rest of the party came to his rescue by grabbing their guns and making an unmistakable "Disposition to Defend themselves and me." The Indians withdrew, but Clark still chose to christen the spot where the unpleasant encounter took place "bad humered Island as we were in a bad humer."[54]

Two months later, hoping to avoid any further misunderstandings, the party took on an interpreter. In November, a

Shortly after purchasing Louisiana, Jefferson put together a team led by Meriwether Lewis and William Clark to explore and document America's new acquisition. Their expedition, the Corps of Discovery (1804–1805), also included an Indian guide, Sacajawea, who smoothed the group's way through Indian lands.

Frenchman named Toussaint Charbonneau appeared and offered his services and those of one of his wives, a young Shoshone woman named Sacajawea. It was she rather than her somewhat unreliable husband who provided the Corps of Discovery with crucial knowledge of the land and the diplomatic skills the little band so desperately needed. Sacajawea's mere presence, with her baby boy Jean Baptiste, helped the explorers avoid trouble. Indians considered a party of men in the company of women and children to have a peaceful intent. Lewis and Clark's journey would have been far more difficult—some might argue impossible—without Sacajawea's help.

Using Sacajawea as a go-between, Lewis and Clark navigated through Indian lands still bounded by culture and lifeways as they had been for centuries. Imperial political borders had never existed here. Thus, in one sense, each meeting between native peoples and the Corps represented a point of contact between the distant past and the near future. New borders would soon be drawn that marked out a national ideology destined to become truly continental, and old lifeways were soon to be extinguished. The Lewis and Clark expedition and its Indian hosts looked out over one place, the Louisiana Territory, but saw two very different worlds.

Lewis and Clark canoed, walked, and climbed their way through a landscape of wonder. Lewis, in April 1805, described the land as "uniformly fertile."[55] Just a few months earlier, he had stood awestruck at the great grasslands, writing that "this senery already rich pleasing and beautiful was farther hightened by immense herds of Buffaloe, deer Elk and Antelopes which we see in every direction feeding on hills and plains." Lewis exclaimed, "I do not think I exaggerate when I estimate the number of Buffaloe which could be compre[hended] at one view to amount to 3000."[56]

By November 1805, the team had reached its objective. Clark made a jubilant entry in the expedition's journal: "We are in view of the Ocian, this great Pacific Octean which we been so long anxious to See. and the roreing or noise made by the waves brakeing on the rockey Shores ... may be heard disti[n]ctly."[57] With that, they turned for home. After 28 months of exploration, the expedition arrived back where their odyssey had begun in September 1806.

Lewis and Clark brought back a storehouse of knowledge. Their scientific observations, descriptions of the natural world, and close study of the Native Americans proved invaluable.

Combined with information gleaned from Zebulon Pike's less celebrated 1806 expedition into the Rocky Mountains, the record of the Corps of Discovery gave Americans their first sense of the place called Louisiana. Here was Thomas Jefferson's "empire of liberty," the vast, open West ready for the plows of yeoman farmers. Here was the stage on which the American drama of vibrant and virtuous democracy, the new American order, would be performed. No longer simply a home, no longer an imperial frontier, Louisiana was about to be transformed into an idea.

7

Americans
and Borders
in Louisiana

The place that Lewis and Clark surveyed and explored so carefully represented the single largest purchase of land in American history prior to the acquisition of Alaska in 1867, a total of just over 800,000 square miles of ground. So much open space naturally attracted farmers, adventurers, and entrepreneurs alike. Small landowners and planters as well as traders and merchants almost instinctively sensed the profit potential of the Louisiana Territory. Soon after the Corps of Discovery returned home, Americans of every ilk began to drift across the Mississippi onto the prairies and into the mountains of the West. Each successive wave brought with it ever grander dreams predicated upon an ideology of inexorable, divinely sanctioned American expansion. The newcomers, moreover, carried a new border concept, even more arbitrary and artificial than the one it replaced. In this new concept, ideology played the starring role. Old boundaries would soon be redrawn according to a set of uniquely American ideas.

The Americanization of the Louisiana Territory began rather quietly. There was no great rush of fortune-seekers that California would later see, only a small coterie of ambitious fur traders. In 1811, a party of traders set up the trading station of Astoria on the Oregon coast. Named after its sponsor and proprietor of the American Fur Company, John Jacob Astor, Astoria was designed to counterbalance the British monopoly in the Pacific Northwest. In this, it was partly successful. Whereas the American Fur Company offered a local alternative to British traders, it lagged behind its competitors in profit and market share. More than a mere presence was needed if the interior fur trade were to be exploited fully.

The real opportunity to surpass the British came in 1822 when businessman and part-time politician William Ashley sent a group of young men up the Missouri to trap and trade. It was he who developed a system whereby the Louisiana Territory could supply the eastern fur and hide markets. Unlike many others, Ashley understood that reciprocal trading with the Indians alone would never satisfy the growing demand in the United

States. The solution, he believed, lay in the organization of an independent contractor system: Americans could fan out along the Louisiana Territory's river valleys and high country woodlands to trap, collect beaver and fox pelts, and sell the product directly to marketers.

Toward this end, Ashley devised the famous rendezvous model in which individual trappers worked on their own, meeting once a year at a predetermined location to sell their furs and

AFTER THE EXPEDITION

The Corps of Discovery returned to a hero's welcome in September 1806 and then promptly faded from the public's mind. Thomas Jefferson rewarded Meriwether Lewis by making him governor of the Louisiana Territory. A good, secure job, the post should have allowed Lewis to live out his life in relative ease. Lewis' short tenure, merely one year, was stormy and ended in his recall to Washington in 1809 to answer charges of mismanagement. Prone to fits of depression, Lewis stopped for the night at an inn near Nashville, Tennessee. There, as far as the evidence can tell, he took his own life. His partner, William Clark, went on to become the United States Indian agent and militia commander for Louisiana. He later took up the post of Missouri's governor prior to statehood; Clark later made an unsuccessful bid to be the state's first governor in 1820. He died in 1838 after a long career as the Superintendent of Indian Affairs. Sacajawea left the Lewis and Clark expedition as it passed through the same villages where she and Charbonneau had first signed on. Her life afterward was plagued by illness and despair. She gave birth to a daughter, Lisette, in 1812 and suddenly died of unknown causes. When Clark heard of his erstwhile interpreter's death, he legally adopted the infant girl and Sacajawea's son, Jean Baptiste. Lisette's fate is unclear, but Jean Baptiste was educated at William Clark's expense and then sent to Europe at the age of 18. Of all the post-Corps of Discovery stories, York's is perhaps the saddest. Treated as an equal and friend by Clark while on the western trails, York once again became human property upon the party's return to the United States. He received neither money nor recognition for his contributions to the expedition's success. Nor did he gain his freedom. Despite his heartfelt pleas, William Clark refused to let York go. He died a slave.

resupply themselves for the coming year. Adopting this system, fur companies were able to nurture a web of solitary agents known collectively as mountain men. Romanticized in popular myth, the mountain men ensured that, by the 1830s, the fur trade boomed throughout the central and northern portions of the Louisiana Territory.

Embodying values and ideals that were quintessentially American, the mountain man served as a transitional figure in the Louisiana Territory's history. The legendary trapper, struggling to survive the rigors of life in the wilderness by combing sharp wits, a steady gun hand, and a knack for forming alliances with local Native Americans, is not entirely a caricature. Men like Jedediah Smith and Jim Bridger were indeed a tough and resourceful bunch, lacking in neither physical fortitude nor keen perception of their own best interests. They often enjoyed good relations with the Indians. They were, however, still products of their generation. No matter how many friendships or working partnerships they forged with local tribes, the mountain men came out of a society that took the American mission for granted; they were harbingers of new concepts about what the land meant. The ideological assumptions the trappers carried into the Louisiana Territory not only supplanted the old imperial view of the place but also foreshadowed the erasure of its earlier Native American counterpart. Put another way, the "mountain men were bicultural [but] not without prejudice." Their activities inaugurated a developmental process "which demoralized, depopulated, and eventually dispossessed the Indians."[58] Because of the mountain men, a new vision of the Louisiana Territory and its borders, however tentative at this early stage, took hold. It remained for other Americans to widen this narrow opening.

Until the 1840s, the mountain men dominated the Rocky Mountains and constituted the largest single American presence over much of the Louisiana Territory. There were two exceptions. Arkansas was well into the process of settlement during the heyday of the fur trade. Located in the well-watered, fertile

James Beckwourth (1798–1867), a Rocky Mountain fur trapper and frontiers-man. Beckwourth, the only African-American fur trapper known to have recorded his life story, *The Life and Adventures of James P. Beckwourth, Mountaineer, Scout, and Pioneer, and Chief of the Crow Nation of Indians* (1856), spun numerous yarns in his autobiography—many of which historians were later able to establish as true. His spirit of adventure embodied that of the typical American frontier adventurer.

southern portion of the territory, Arkansas drew farmers and planters from the State of Louisiana below it and the southeastern states across the Mississippi. Looking for prime cotton land, similar to that in the states of Mississippi and Alabama but less crowded, slave-owning growers settled in Arkansas in numbers large enough to qualify it for statehood in 1836. That Arkansas would be a slave state no one doubted and no one disputed even though slavery had never existed there. Arkansas lay below a cartographic fiction known as the Missouri Compromise Line, perhaps the most significant internal arbitrary border in nineteenth-century America.

The area just on the other side of the Mississippi River from Arkansas had belonged to the Cherokee, Choctaw, Chickasaw, and Creek Indians. Along with the Seminole of Florida, these groups made up the so-called Five Civilized Tribes, thus named because they had chosen peaceful coexistence and cultural assimilation as the means by which to keep their ancestral lands. They succeeded well enough until 1830 when President Andrew Jackson pushed the Indian Removal Act through Congress. The act called for the expulsion of the Five Civilized Tribes from their homeland and their resettlement across the Mississippi to the western fringe of the Louisiana Territory, in modern-day Oklahoma. Only after this tragic eviction could white migration into the Deep South proceed in earnest, unhindered by the just claims of the land's rightful owners. It was not long before latecomers, denied the opportunity to buy choice acreage for their slaves to work, crossed the river into Arkansas.

A similar process to the north brought farmers, and their slaves, from Kentucky and Tennessee into Missouri. Nestled between the Missouri and Mississippi rivers, the fertile soil in Missouri attracted men who had an excess of labor but too little land. Using the city of St. Louis as a river port, anyone tilling the ground in Missouri had a good chance at success, even more so if the people doing the work never had to be paid. By 1820, the number of inhabitants in Missouri qualified it for statehood; the fact that most of these people owned slaves meant that Missouri would petition for entrance as a slave state.

Here the problems began. Allowing Missouri to enter the Union with slavery threatened to upset the delicate balance between slave and free states in the United States Congress, a balance that had made it possible for politicians in Washington to avoid any serious discussion of slavery's role in the nation's life and society. Missouri statehood promised a bitter legislative fight or worse. One member of Congress, Speaker of the House Henry Clay, ominously predicted that this "most unhappy question" of Missouri statehood might even lead to armed conflict. Clay lamented that, in the House of Representatives, words such as "civil war and disunion, are uttered almost without emotion."[59]

It is not surprising that Clay took a leading role in working out a compromise. Acting in concert with other members of Congress, Clay put together a deal that recognized the reality of slavery in Missouri while maintaining the balance of political power between North and South. The Missouri Compromise, as it came to be called, provided for Missouri's admission as a slave state in exchange for Maine's simultaneous entry as a free state. This done, Clay and his partners moved to prevent such disputes in the future. Congress extended the Mason-Dixon Line, which separated Pennsylvania and Maryland and had acted for decades as the informal border between the free North and the slave South, straight through the Louisiana Territory. Running along the latitudinal line of 36° 30′, the Missouri Compromise Line set the most important criterion for determining how new states would join the Union. Above the line, except for the newly admitted States of Missouri, a state would be free; below it, slavery was the rule. Proud of their achievement, however stopgap, the compromisers congratulated themselves but never really reflected on the implications of their deal in terms of border formation in the Louisiana Territory.

In 1821, the same year that Missouri entered the Union, the United States ratified the revised version of a two-year-old treaty with Spain. The terms of the treaty gave the United States possession of Florida, something it had sought for years, and substantial land transfers in southeastern Texas and in the area between the Red and Arkansas Rivers. Again, the United States grew larger. More importantly, the treaty ended a nettlesome and long-lingering dispute over the exact location of the border between the Louisiana Territory and the Spanish northern provinces. Once and for all, everyone knew what belonged to the decaying Spanish Empire and what could be claimed the young United States. With the Transcontinental Treaty, also known as the Adams–Onis Treaty after its American and Spanish architects, the ultimate transition from the imperial to the ideological models of border creation had begun. The old conception of borders as political ramparts erected between imperial competitors gave way to one based on a developing sense of American identity and national mission.

Missouri's state boundaries were the first real internal political borders the Louisiana Territory had ever known other than the administrative lines drawn by Jefferson's government just after the purchase.[60] The boundary lines of the imperial period had always been outer-directed, defining what lay outside of them. Now internal political divisions partitioned space viewed previously as a single unit by the European powers that had held it. Even the Native Americans had looked at Louisiana as one contiguous space, culturally shared and apportioned but fundamentally indivisible. By blending elements of these two models and by introducing ideology into the mix, the United States broke new ground. Although it was designed primarily to separate two increasingly divergent and antagonistic cultures, one predicated on slavery and another based on freedom, the Missouri Compromise created a novel scheme for political division. More than that, the line it established compelled a reevaluation of just what American continental expansion would look like and exactly which ideas would serve as its motive force.

A unified people and nation were supposed to recreate the Louisiana Territory in their own republican image. The virgin West was where Jefferson's mythical "empire of liberty" would be extended and elaborated. No one anticipated an ideological rupture caused by slavery or by the arbitrary border separating those areas with it and those without. An elderly Jefferson described the "Missouri question" as "a fire-bell in the night" that "awakened and filled [him] with terror." Clay's compromise line, Jefferson wrote, was "a reprieve only, not a final sentence."

The former president feared for his beloved country and put little faith in an imaginary line as a cure for its fundamental ideological ailments: "A geographical line, coinciding with a marked principle, moral and political, once conceived ... will never be obliterated; and every new irritation will mark it deeper and deeper."[61]

Beginning with the crisis surrounding Missouri's petition for statehood, Americans began to wonder just whose ideas would shape the future of the United States in general and the Louisiana Territory in particular. Political borders and cultural boundaries took on new meaning and gravity in the charged atmosphere of the slavery debate. Violence did not trail far behind.

Missouri and Arkansas emerged out of the Louisiana Territory in the opening stages of a new type of internal organization. Ordinary people and their politicians scrutinized the Louisiana Territory for signs of the next ideological clash between freedom and slavery. This did not mean that they were blind to the territory's external borders—far from it. The dividing line between the United States and Mexico was a matter of contention and that with British Canada was still partially undetermined. Along thousands of miles, claims and counterclaims about where the borders were and what belonged to whom vied with one another. Notwithstanding domestic quarrels like the one over Missouri, American expansionism continued unabated into the 1840s, straining relations with Great Britain and with Mexico.

Spain never had to endure the pressure of American expansion as Mexico did. Newly independent in 1821, Mexico found itself confronted by an aggressive northern neighbor that conceived of borders as ideological frontiers. The United States felt secure in the belief that it was the country's "manifest destiny," as editor John L. O'Sullivan termed it in 1839, to roll across the Louisiana Territory all the way to California, spreading "the excellence of divine principles" along the way. O'Sullivan and many of his countrymen believed that God had chosen the

United States "to establish on earth moral dignity and the salvation of man." He promised that the United States "shall smite unto death" those imperial "kings, hierarchs, and oligarchs" who got in its way.[62] Mexico, it seemed, had been warned.

Mexico parried this ideological thrust as best it could. It first tried to absorb the blow by welcoming American immigrants into Texas and California, in much the same way that the British had tolerated a growing American presence in the disputed Oregon Country. Accommodation rather than conflict seemed to offer a fledgling Mexico its best defense against American infiltration. Mexico's border with the United States was without a doubt a political boundary. Mexico recognized clear cultural differences between itself and its geographic antagonist, but no ideology comparable to the American one influenced its international relations. Mexican policymakers fatally underestimated the threat posed by the United States, especially American citizens who were allowed into Mexico's northern provinces. Trouble arose, coming to a climax in the 1836 Texas rebellion.

The engine driving the westward movement of America's external border had always been the pervasive belief that God had a special purpose for the United States. In taking that for granted, no obstacle could be tolerated—neither an imperial bully such as Great Britain, which jealously guarded Canadian interests in Oregon, nor a racial "other" such as Mexico, which prevented the spread of American ideals to the West. The Louisiana Purchase had ended the French Empire in North America permanently. In the process, it had doubled the size of the nation. Now the time had come to peel Mexico and Britain off the territory's borders. Both countries were remnants of a bygone day that did little more than impede the flow of the new order of the ages being constructed by the United States. One way or another, they had to go.

Britain went first. The Oregon Treaty of 1846 gave Louisiana a secure northern border and added Oregon to America's western lands. American territory now stretched unbroken from the Mississippi to the Pacific, at least in the north. To the south,

Mexico blocked the way, and it was toward that direction that Americans turned next. The border Mexico claimed with the United States had been shared peacefully by Spain and France for almost 100 years. The Mexican government had respected the same boundary since 1821, and it is not surprising that Mexico was shocked by the warlike posture struck by the United States in 1846. Public opinion, in some sectors, favored absorbing Mexico in its entirety. Referred to at times as the "all-Mexico movement," these people advocated not just a continental but a hemispheric United States. A southern border that encompassed the whole of Mexico, if not all of Central America, was envisioned by the most radical of these proponents who, not coincidentally, favored the introduction of slavery into any areas acquired by the United States.

Such rabid expansionists remained in the distinct minority. Nonetheless, President Polk moved aggressively to redefine the old border. After annexing Texas, which had never been part of the Louisiana Territory, a year earlier, it seemed only logical to the Polk administration that the established Red River borderline should be extended southward to the Rio Grande. The Mexicans, operating on the old buffer model inherited from Spain, claimed the smaller Nueces River as Mexico's border with Texas and the United States, thus putting some distance between the United States and Mexico proper. When the United States insisted on the Rio Grande as an international boundary, Mexico responded by moving its army toward Texas. This decision cost the Mexicans dearly in the end, but they had few other viable alternatives given the Americans' ideological-territorial convictions.

Primed for a fight, American and Mexican troops clashed along the Rio Grande in May 1846, giving President Polk the excuse he needed to declare war. The short but sharp conflict that followed resulted in the seizure of California and the effective defeat of Mexico in September 1847. Five months later, in the town of Guadalupe Hidalgo, the United States and Mexico finalized a treaty that ended the war and gave the United States all it wanted. The whole of the Mexican north was transferred to American control, sweeping away the last of the old imperial borders. A line that had stood for over 150 years disappeared in an instant.

The Oregon Treaty and the Treaty of Guadalupe Hidalgo brought a definitive close to the imperial phase of the Louisiana Territory's external borders. Native Americans drew distinctions and fluid boundaries between themselves based on differing lifeways and concrete, material relationships with the land itself. Europeans constructed more arbitrary borders based on imperial politics that represented even greater abstractions than the cultural demarcations of the Native Americans. Now the Americans had arrived, carrying their ideology of a divine mission to plant democracy across the continent. Ironically, that ideology was about to turn on itself. The Louisiana Territory was soon to become a field for battles between competing interpretations of manifest destiny. Whether or not the "empire of liberty" would contain slaves was the question. In the process of coming up with an answer, the Louisiana Territory would begin to fade away, but only after the worst period of bloodshed in American history.

8

Blood on
the Land

Except for California, with its fertile San Joaquin Valley, soon-to-be-bustling port of San Francisco, and the Sierra foothills laden with gold, most of the land acquired from Mexico in 1848 did not amount to much. The largest parts of it consisted of rugged mountains, barren sinks, and lonely deserts. The place was sparsely populated outside of the old Spanish settlements, mostly by small groups of resolute and resilient Native Americans. Not much promise could be found there.

The Louisiana Territory, through which emigrants had been trekking westward in increasing numbers, was a completely different story. On the prairies, the creation of an entirely new set of arbitrary, abstract borders began in earnest in the 1850s. Culture and politics would provide a loose framework for these imaginary lines, but ideology remained the primary impulse behind them. They represented an ideological breakdown. What had once been a unifying feature of American society, namely a national purpose, had split into two warring segments. The lever that pried them apart was slavery.

Missouri had been only the opening act in a tragedy unlike anything the nation had ever seen. From 1820 onward, the question of slavery's status in newly organized territory complicated what had been a relatively straightforward ideological discussion of national growth and the spread of democratic institutions. People had spoken of manifest destiny as a vague set of closely related ideas regarding where the nation was meant to go in general. The idea of spreading American values remained constant, but which values should be spread? Slavery and freedom both existed in the American model. Which one would shape the new territories across the Mississippi? As long as the issue could be skirted, no one dared to discuss openly the extent to which slavery would follow along as the country moved west. Debate, where it occurred at all, had been generally muted. Few seemed willing to raise such a divisive issue in the public forum. Missouri and the Mexican cession forced the matter. The expansionist creed remained unchallenged; the sticking point now was the future role of slavery.

Nowhere were the contours of this national disagreement marked out as boldly as in the very center of the Louisiana Territory, where the land was ripe for the plow and the future was as open as the horizon. Near the confluence of the Missouri and Mississippi rivers, the soil beckoned. Once a plow capable of tearing through the tough sod had been invented, the area drew thousands of farmers. The agricultural potential of the region was virtually unlimited, but the territory would have to be organized before it could be exploited. Louisiana had to be carved into smaller territories and then states, all of which would need constitutions, governments, and laws. These new political entities would also have to wrestle with the slavery problem.

Missouri had resolved the problem to an extent, but the line that resulted from the statehood compromise, as Jefferson had predicted, etched the differences between free state and slave state adherents all the more deeply. The explanation was rather simple. Perhaps no borderline drawn in American history was more fictitious than that provided for in the Missouri Compromise. Essentially a crude extension of the Mason-Dixon Line, the Missouri line that bisected the Louisiana Territory followed no natural feature at all; it cut across open space without logic or reason. Only a last minute compromise over California statehood prevented this abstraction from continuing on to the Pacific. Despite its utter lack of any real meaning, the 36° 30′ line appeared boldly on maps of the Louisiana Territory. It quickly became a fiercely contested and easily erasable ideological border.

The Americans who moved in to settle the Louisiana Territory did so for myriad reasons, but the foundation upon which their interests and agendas had been built consisted first and foremost of ideas. These ideas spoke to people about who they were and what they deserved as a nation with a "manifest destiny." The ideological inconsistencies that developed here led one group of Americans to see a future of free yeoman farmers tilling the soil and the other to envision a land where a man's property, even human property, was sacred. The end result was a storm of violence that broke in 1854.

Senator Stephen Douglas, a gifted orator, committed his home state of Illinois to building a railway between Chicago and San Franciso. To facilitate this venture, Douglas submitted to Congress in 1854 a bill known as the Kansas–Nebraska Act. The bill designated the settlement of the Louisiana Territory, necessary for the successful railroad venture. Under this Act, Kansas and Nebraska would be organized as separate federal territories, and when they were ready to be admitted to the Union as states, the residents of the states would decide whether the states would be slave or free. The Act led to the abolishment of the Missouri Compromise Line.

The line Henry Clay helped craft in 1820 held for 34 years until a combination of population growth and a keen desire to lay a railroad to California made reorganizing the Louisiana Territory into separate, smaller territories an urgent matter. The territory had to be fully integrated into the national economic system if it were to be utilized profitably. Political division followed by a railroad, or better yet several railroads, offered the best plan for realizing the genuine value of the place. No politician recognized this more readily or acted with greater purpose than Stephen Douglas. As Illinois's voice in the Senate, the short but intense Douglas was known for his booming oratory. Indeed, it had earned him the nickname "the Little Giant." Keeping a sharp eye on the interests of his home state, Douglas committed himself to forging a railroad connection between Chicago and San Francisco. The problem was the Louisiana Territory. Half of its space had yet to be organized, a crucial prerequisite for a rail link. The areas to the north and west of Missouri sat blank on the map.

Eager to fill up that space with territories through which a railroad profiting Illinois might run, Douglas submitted a bill to Congress in 1854. After much debate, the bill passed both the Senate and House and became the Kansas–Nebraska Act. Under its provisions, Kansas and Nebraska were to be organized as separate federal territories, with the latter encompassing everything from Missouri to the Canadian border. The key part of the legislation dealt with statehood for all or part of the new territories. When ready, according to the requirements of the U.S. Constitution, states forming out of Kansas and Nebraska would be admitted as free or slave on the basis of popular sovereignty. As the act put it, its purpose was "to leave the people [of the territories] perfectly free to form and regulate their domestic institutions in their own way." It stated explicitly that "nothing herein contained shall be construed to revive or put into force any law or regulation ... either protecting, establishing, prohibiting, or abolishing slavery."[63] Essentially, the people of a new state had the privilege of choosing to live with or without slavery; no reference to the Missouri Compromise Line needed to be made.

The doctrine of popular sovereignty represented a feeble and rather transparent attempt to sidestep the issue of slavery and stave off a clash over its expansion into the Louisiana Territory. Douglas hoped to settle the matter by avoiding it; in the end, his legislative sleight-of-hand succeeded in accomplishing neither feat. The Kansas-Nebraska Act exacerbated existing tension by dissolving the Missouri Compromise Line. Admittedly, the line itself had been little more than a convenient fiction, a comforting illusion that no one seriously expected to last forever. Arkansas had entered the Union under its provisions without incident, as had Texas and Iowa. Thus the line functioned at least minimally to prevent disputes like the one over Missouri. Douglas's bill, however, crippled it in this crucial respect. With this illusory but operational internal border now all but defunct, violence became the arbiter of the contest over slavery in the Louisiana Territory.

Freed from the constraints of the 36° 30′ line, Kansas petitioned for statehood first. In March 1855, the newly appointed territorial governor ordered an election to put in place a legislature, preparatory to drafting a state constitution. The voting rapidly degenerated into an unseemly political debacle. Pro-slavery men from Missouri, the infamous "border ruffians," poured into Kansas, stuffed ballot boxes, and tipped the decision toward slave-state proponents. Free-state Kansans promptly declared the election to be invalid and the resulting legislature a fraud. The antislavery camp did more than protest. It set up a rival government in the town of Topeka.

Denied an appeal to the Missouri Compromise Line, Kansas split in two. With opposing governments in place, as one historian observed, "the polarization of forces in Kansas was almost complete. The population was divided into two groups, each group armed to the teeth."[64] The situation grew worse as the months passed. By early 1856, both sides had made up their minds to settle with guns what they could not settle with ballots. Kansas exploded in open warfare. Striking the first major blow, slave-staters launched a vicious attack in May against the town of Lawrence. The mob burned buildings, including the home of the free-state governor, destroyed the local newspaper, and even brought up cannons to shell the town's largest hotel. One man died during the raid. Free-staters returned the favor later in the month. Fuming over the "Lawrence massacre," arch-abolitionist John Brown and his sons butchered five suspected pro-slavery farmers along the Pottawatomie Creek. With first blood spilled, both camps settled in for what each believed would be a long fight.

The bitter conflict raged for months, fueled on the slave-state side by fighters from Missouri and on the other by men and guns from the East, primarily New England. Over time, the free-state faction gained the advantage. Although their support came from far away, it came in abundance. Guns were smuggled into Kansas by front groups such as the New England Emigrant Aid Society. Many sympathetic Northeasterners openly declared their intent to encourage the violence if it meant that Kansas would be free of slaves. Even religious leaders became involved.

Prominent minister Henry Ward Beecher, for example, publicly condoned sending arms to Kansas and did his part by seeing to it that shipments of Sharps rifles arrived in crates marked "Bibles." The breech-loading rifles were nicknamed "Beecher's Bibles."

By the beginning of 1857, a series of free-state victories and the arrival of a new, energetic governor, not to mention the federal troops he brought with him, helped bring the level of violence down. Kansans began slowly to pick up the pieces of their shattered territory. A total of 200 people had died and over $2 million in property had been destroyed. Kansas statehood was denied. It would not be granted until 1861, just in time for a much bloodier civil war.

The prominent northeastern minister and abolitionist Henry Ward Beecher. Favorite brother of Harriet Beecher Stowe (author of the antislavery novel *Uncle Tom's Cabin*), Beecher advocated violence as a way to settle the slavery issue, sending shipments of Sharps rifles to Kansas to aid the cause. Because the guns arrived in crates marked "Bibles," they came to be known as "Beecher's Bibles."

The fighting in Kansas was a direct consequence of the legislative erasure of the Missouri Compromise Line. It can be argued that the Congress merely exposed a preexisting and fatal flaw in the line—it had never really been there to begin with. The line was a political attempt to use an arbitrary border to solve an ideological problem. It certainly did not conform to any natural features or relationships nor did it identify any genuine cultural differences. It was intended to keep slavery's proponents and opponents at bay. Even the mere hope that such a fictional divide might successfully wall off one antagonistic set of ideas from another was totally naïve. Like so many other borders around

U.S. Chief Justice Roger Taney, who argued the Dred Scott decision in 1857. Taney held that slaves were not citizens and could not sue in federal courts, and that per provisions of the U.S. Constitution, Congress could not forbid slavery in the territories of the United States, and in fact could not legally confine slavery to the South. Taney's decision nullified the Mason-Dixon and Missouri Compromise lines and established the battleground for the fight about slavery.

the world, the line's arbitrary characteristics not only made it vulnerable to trespass but also exaggerated exactly the differences it was intended to settle. Simply drawing a line on a map and admonishing people to honor it attracted more attention to the issue, not less, and underscored the irreconcilable differences that would inevitably lead to war.

The argument over which ideas would shape the future of the United States had, by this point, moved beyond the ability of imaginary lines to contain it. The Kansas-Nebraska Act had essentially opened the entire Louisiana Territory to slavery while allowing people in parts of the territory to vote it away. This held true until the Supreme Court stepped in. Given the case of a slave, Dred Scott, who claimed to be free in light of his being taken at one time into free territory, the Court wiped the Missouri Compromise Line from the map. Not content with Stephen Douglas's expedient of popular sovereignty, the Supreme Court ruled in the case of Dred Scott that no compromise line, arbitrary or not, could stop the spread of slavery. Writing for the court, Chief Justice Roger Taney argued that the Missouri Compromise had effectively prohibited slavery "in that part of the territory ceded by France, under the name of Louisiana," an outcome not justified by the Constitution. In fact,

Taney concluded, the exclusion of slavery from "the territory of the United States" north of the 36° 30′ line "is not warranted by the Constitution, and is therefore void."[65]

The Dred Scott decision ruled that no border could legally confine slavery to the South. Laws that had previously excluded slaves from various states and territories were struck down. The Mason-Dixon Line vanished; the Missouri Compromise Line dissolved; even popular sovereignty was consigned to the musty corners of history. Politicians and their constituents alike had shared the delusion of arbitrary borders as saviors of the peace, guarantors of a status quo in which slavery and freedom coexisted, however fitfully. The nation had agreed to pretend that fictional lines could make a fundamental ideological conflict go away. Dred Scott shattered the illusions of a generation and promised to extend the battleground of the slavery question far beyond Kansas and Missouri to the rest of the country.

The final rupture between North and South came in April 1861. The war that followed consumed over 600,000 American lives. It cut long swaths of destruction across the land. Farms were ravaged and cities burned. No one failed to feel in some way the fiery touch of war. Although concentrated east of the Mississippi, the fighting recognized no boundaries. Indeed, it made a mockery of the very same arbitrary borders that had partly caused the conflict in the first place.

Missouri, Kansas, and Arkansas, as a result, soon saw their share of the fighting. Only two months after Confederate soldiers fired on the federal base at Fort Sumter, situated on an island outside of Charleston, South Carolina, combat erupted in Missouri. Although a slave state, not all of its citizens favored secession; unlike other Southern states, Missouri did not immediately leave the Union either in the wake of Abraham Lincoln's election or after the shooting war began. Unionists and secessionists took to their respective sides and began killing one another. Union triumphs in a series of skirmishes and pitched battles throughout the state eventually drove out Confederate troops and sympathizers, who retreated into Arkansas, and opened the way for the installation of a solidly Unionist state government by the end of July.

The establishment of firm political control over Missouri, however, did not translate into peace. With a few exceptions, uniformed forces engaging in open battles were almost never seen in Missouri and Kansas; instead, rival militias took to the field. These ragged bands of undisciplined irregulars grappled with one another in some of the most vicious, merciless fighting of the entire war. Guerilla outfits nominally supporting either the Confederacy or the Union sprang up all over Missouri. Often crossing into outright banditry, these units raided farms and towns at will in a fit of unrestrained murder, arson, and robbery that reminded many of the violence of 1856. Indeed, as Emory Thomas wrote, the "war in western Missouri and eastern Kansas was ... a continuation of the raiding and bushwhacking that which had been going on there since the mid-1850s."[66] Confederate "bushwhackers" such as William Quantrill and "Bloody Bill" Anderson, not to mention Frank and Jesse James, terrorized Missouri and ranged into Kansas, bringing death and mayhem in the name of Southern liberty. Their dark exertions were matched by pro-Union Kansas "jayhawkers" who were led by commanders like James Lane and James Montgomery. No line circumscribed the fighting between the militias; the so-called border between Missouri and Kansas was crossed with abandon. The former endured the greatest hardship in the end. "Missouri suffered the horrors of internecine warfare," historian James McPherson concluded, "and the resulting hatreds which persisted for decades after" the end of the Civil War.[67]

Except for Pea Ridge at the beginning (1862) and the battle of Westport (1864) near the end of the war, the fighting in Missouri never matched the scale of that in the East or even that just across the Mississippi River in Tennessee and in the state of Mississippi. The battle of Prairie Grove (Arkansas) and the capture of New Orleans by Union gunboats, both in 1862, were crucial to Union victory, but in terms of men engaged, they did not even approach other more famous engagements in Virginia and

Pennsylvania. Nevertheless, it was the ongoing guerilla war in the old Louisiana Territory that marked the climax of the ideological struggle to define what it meant to be an American. This was a contest without the cover of flags and uniforms, a true people's war.

A WAR WITHIN A WAR

While the armies of the Union and Confederacy battled one another on the bloody battlefields of the East, war laid a heavy hand on the Louisiana Territory. Standard accounts of the Civil War discuss the "West" in the context of Ulysses Grant's Mississippi campaign of 1862–1863, naval combat on the Mississippi River, and the major engagements in Arkansas and Missouri. As Alvin Josephy pointed out so well in his 1991 book, *The Civil War in the American West*, there was far more going on than this. Josephy argued that historians have for too long overlooked "everything west of the Union campaigns to secure Missouri and the Mississippi River," and have left the public woefully ignorant of "the events of the conflict in the western sections of the nation."[*] He could not have been more accurate.

The West formed a much broader theater of operations than has been suggested. Texas and New Mexico saw formal combat between Union and Confederate armies, but fighting also took place in the Dakotas, Wyoming, Minnesota, and Oklahoma. Here, federal troops engaged in bitter contests with Native Americans who were either openly or indirectly supporting the Confederacy. At the very least, many Indians hoped for better treatment in a land where whites were divided amongst themselves. Many Indian tribes in Oklahoma expressed their aspirations by organizing units to fight as Confederate auxiliaries, such as Stand Watie's Cherokee Confederate Provisional Army, or by putting together guerilla bands to raid Union supply depots, cut Federal communications, and ambush troop convoys. Even in areas where neither the U.S. soldiers nor the Indians had much stake in the war taking place further east, pitched battles were waged along the trails and passes leading through the Rocky Mountains. Regardless of the form it took, the war as it was fought throughout the Louisiana Territory lacked in neither bitterness nor significance.

[*] Alvin M. Josephy, Jr., *The Civil War in the American West.* New York: Random House, 1991, p. xi.

Ideas brought the United States to Louisiana; initially, ideas about manifest destiny, and later, ideas about slavery. This process led inevitably to the erection of borders and the drawing of lines that were at once arbitrary and totally abstract. Culture, politics, and genuine relationships with the land could be found, certainly, but these represented vestigial elements of days long gone. From 1861 to 1865, Americans fought over utterly imaginary lines. When the gunfire ceased, the disputes over these lines had been settled and slavery was abolished. The nation had been made physically, socially, and, most of all, ideologically whole. The creed of progress, soon to animate industry, fill cities, and pull in immigrants from abroad, "ordained by God" and implemented by free hands, had triumphed. A single America, a truly "United" States, spanned the continent. With its breakup into new territories and states, the Louisiana Territory lost its distinctiveness and blended into this larger republic; in fact, it ceased to exist politically. The old Native American boundaries and imperial borders now shared the pages of history books with the abstract, ideological lines that had once defined the Louisiana Territory.

A tragic last act still had to be played out. A melancholy epilogue remained to be written. Ironically, the rise of borders divorced from any sort of concrete ties to the land and detached from the type of political significance they had once carried brought two visions of Louisiana into a final conflict. The newest view of Louisiana met the oldest head-on. Even as the United States tore at itself in civil war, the government was busy designing a system of enclosures, artificially and arbitrarily bounded spaces called reservations, in which to place the last remnants of America's native peoples.

From 1864 to 1890, men, women, and children steeped in a tradition of fluid borders defining concrete natural relationships were forced onto tiny plots of land, enclaves surrounded by imaginary lines. The story of what happened whenever and wherever these borders were transgressed stands as a sad closure to the tale of the Louisiana Territory.

9

A Clash
in Time

On the morning of November 29, 1864, Methodist minister and former Kansas guerilla Colonel John M. Chivington ordered his 700-man mounted detachment to charge into a Cheyenne village along the banks of Sand Creek in Colorado. Within the group of tepees, fires smoldered; here and there an occasional dog scavenged for food. Unaware of the impending danger, 500 Indians slept secure in the notion that they had nothing to fear from the white soldiers. The villagers had no reason to suspect trouble; their leaders had just finished negotiating a peace with Chivington himself. In fact, an American flag hung from the chief's tepee. Nevertheless, the soldiers came, thundering through the still morning air.

When the colonel and his troopers finally left, the camp was in ruins and more than 200 Indians, mostly women and young children, lay dead. Their only offense had been their adherence to a way of life and a way of looking at the land that had long since been eclipsed by more modern perceptions. As the 3rd Regiment returned to Denver, a local newspaper exulted, "Colorado soldiers have again covered themselves with glory."[68] Some time later, the scalps of many of the Indians who had died at Sand Creek were put on public exhibition in a crowded Denver theater, much to the amazement and amusement of the audience.[69]

The Sand Creek massacre inaugurated a war of annihilation between the first and the latest inhabitants of the Louisiana Territory. For the next 45 years, the land was darkened by the shadow of inhuman brutality and wanton slaughter. A racial war of the bloodiest kind rolled across the plains, a war precipitated by lines that set out in the starkest terms two mutually exclusive ways of seeing the rivers, mountains, and prairies Jefferson had purchased in 1803.

Native Americans viewed the land as a sustaining and sustainable ecosystem with which humans could forge a material relationship. Their border concept was structured accordingly. Men like Chivington saw the land as an extension of a set of ideas relating to progress, modernity, and a future dominated by arbitrary lines marking out states and federal territories totally divorced from the natural world. That these lines would be drawn in the interests of the United States government seemed perfectly legitimate, considering the "fact" that God smiled uniquely on the nation. As Robert M. Utley has asserted, "At the heart of the land issue lay starkly differing attitudes toward land."[70] The government saw it as property, whereas the Indians saw it as a web of relationships. Nature was everything to them, but nature had nothing to do with the boundary lines that would soon finish the process of carving up and disposing of the last hints of the Louisiana Territory.

Native Americans rarely understood and never fully accepted the validity of boundaries created without any reference to the natural world. They were even more routinely baffled by the notion that such fictions might apply to them and their world. Imaginary borders might direct the actions of the "white man," but never their own. It was, therefore, with confusion and dismay that Native Americans watched as the United States government moved to confine them within the artificial spaces "reserved" for them. The Indians at first rejected the very thought of living out their lives on reservations created by an alien culture. As time progressed, however, it became apparent that the old ways were passing. Although many Native Americans resisted valiantly, in the end, the borders drawn on government maps prevailed, and the evolutionary process that had begun in Louisiana centuries earlier came to an end.

The idea of relegating Indians to remote parcels of strictly circumscribed land was not new. Andrew Jackson had forcibly evicted the Five Civilized Tribes in the 1830s, herding them across the Mississippi along the Trail of Tears. Jackson justified his actions at the time in terms that people of Chivington's generation accepted as self-evident. The president told Congress that Native Americans were incorrigible, "they can not [sic] live in contact with a civilized community." Their day had passed and the Indians had to make way for a new way of understanding America. "The past we can not recall, but the future we can provide for," Jackson said.⁷¹ That future put the great Southern tribes far from home, in what was then called Indian Territory and is today Oklahoma.

Thirty years after the completion of Jackson's resettlement scheme, the Civil War ended. Americans welcomed the relief from the bloodletting between North and South without noticing that another war still raged in the West. It began in 1862 when the Sioux in Minnesota rose up after being denied food promised by the U.S. government, an agent of which remarked, "So far as I am concerned if [the Indians] are hungry let them eat grass or their own dung."⁷² The ensuing struggle spread

RESERVATIONS TODAY

Over 70 Indian reservations dot the former Louisiana Territory. Many are located in Oklahoma, the first portion of the territory to receive displaced Native Americans in the 1830s. Until 1907, Oklahoma was the largest single tract of land given over exclusively to Indian occupation, but today, both the Dakotas and Montana also contain sizable reservations. The total population of the reservations in the area Louisiana once covered is over 400,000. The borders these people live within are essentially political; they define relationships between the Native Americans and the state and federal governments rather than specific lifeways or cultures. Notwithstanding continual efforts to revive, recreate, or simply maintain the vestigial elements of ancient traditions, the reservation system is not designed with the old ways in mind. Its primary function is to wrap political borders around indigenous peoples, in effect replicating the imperial boundaries of the seventeenth and eighteenth centuries. The penetration of the reservations by the broader social and cultural patterns of the United States is in keeping with the third, ideological, phase of the Louisiana Territory's evolution. Native Americans, despite a determination to retain a distinct identity, are fully integrated into the larger American system and operate by its rules, except perhaps in the limited sense of local community life. Reservations today, in particular those in the old purchase area, represent a synthesis of better than 300 years worth of change and differing ways of looking at the land.

across the grasslands, involving all of the major tribes—the Kiowa, Comanche, Arapahoe, and Cheyenne. For the next five years, Indians and soldiers fought one another to a draw. The killing stopped in October 1867, when the two sides came to an agreement at Medicine Creek Lodge in Kansas.

Medicine Creek Lodge set a precedent. The tribes involved agreed to move to reservations in exchange for food, arms, and guaranteed land tenure. Such offers became commonplace in the years to come, creating divisions between those Indians who were willing to accept a life within arbitrary lines and those who were not. Some members of various tribes proved willing to let go of their traditional relationship with the land, but many others recognized that such surrender meant the end of lifeways that had provided them with a coherent identity, a sense of self as individuals and as a distinct people. These men and women remained defiant and asserted their right to define their own borders as they saw fit.

Indians of this sort refused to lock themselves on the reservations like the one set up near the Black Hills of the Dakota Territory under the terms of the agreement reached at Fort Laramie, Wyoming, in the spring of 1868. A companion to the one drawn up at Medicine Creek, the Fort Laramie treaty made extensive concessions to the Sioux in return for acceptance of permanent resettlement on a huge government reservation that included prime hunting lands and unfettered access to the sacred Black Hills.

Most of the Sioux covered by the Fort Laramie accord respected its provisions in their own way. Even though many groups eagerly accepted government food rations, they never fully adjusted to reservation life. Especially among the Oglala and Hunkpapa Sioux, the Northern Cheyenne, and the Northern Arapahoe, the connections between the Indians and the reservation remained tenuous. Robert Utley has commented that the commitment of many restless Native Americans "wavered with the seasons." When food was scarce, retreat to the reservations and their food stores was a distasteful necessity, but

General George Armstrong Custer, a dashing, reckless Civil War veteran anxious to fight Indians, was sent in June 1876 to force the last of the free Indians to move onto a reservation. Custer's view of the American Indian was that "as he is, and so far as knowledge goes, as he has ever been, [he is] a savage in every sense of the word." Custer met with Indian resistance in his endeavor, mainly because his expedition into the Black Hills of the Dakota Territory, during which he discovered gold on Indian lands, involved trespass-  ing onto the hunting grounds and sacred burial grounds of the Great Sioux Reservation. Chief Sitting Bull and his warriors, camped by the Little Big Horn River in Montana, greatly outnumbered Custer and his men, and because of his miscalculation, Custer and his regiment were wiped out during the attack.

when the buffalo herds appeared, the hunters left, having "no intention of abandoning the free life of the chase for the dubious attractions of the reservation."[73]

These rebellious spirits mocked those Indians who gave up the ways of their ancestors. Rather than following the herds and observing boundaries of their own design, the reservation Indians had sold their souls. As the famous Hunkpapa chief Sitting Bull said, "You [reservation Indians] are fools to make yourselves slaves to a piece of fat bacon, some hard-tack, and a little sugar and coffee."[74] It came as no surprise that Sitting Bull led the way off the reservation when the time came to resist change on the Great Plains.

The Native Americans who rejected reservation life and its federally defined arbitrary borders chose to follow an older path. For them, "their" land was any they chose to hunt upon, and they did not readily tolerate trespassers. The off-reservation groups carried their boundaries with their tepees. At the same time, settlers and miners in the region rarely respected the borders drawn by the U.S. government, let alone those claimed by "savages." Conflict over who could rightfully be where was inevitable.

The people who came West in the last decades of the nineteenth century respected neither the native peoples nor their ideas about the land. Hunting buffalo and following the rhythms of nature did not interest them at all. Nature, in fact, was the adversary of the newcomers. The great grasses were to be cleared, the buffalo wiped out, and the Indians dispossessed. All would be replaced with farms and farmers, cattle, towns, and states. The white migrants longed for the day when "the grass would be gone with the buffalo and the Indian."[75]

Land rights based on tradition had no resonance with people who applied the label American exclusively to themselves. They were agents of progress, and progress went hand in hand with profit. This might mean farming or ranching or building railroads; it might also mean mining for copper, lead, silver, and, of course, gold. It was during an expedition led by George Armstrong Custer that gold was discovered in the Black Hills in 1874.

Custer was a dashing, reckless Civil War veteran who followed his old cavalry commander, Philip Sheridan, west after the war ended. On the plains, Custer hoped to win glory and promotions; he wanted a real military career. Flamboyant and supremely confident, Custer savored the opportunity to fight Indians. Native Americans, in Custer's opinion, were anything but the "simple-minded 'son of nature,' desiring nothing beyond the privilege of roaming and hunting over the vast unsettled wilds of the West" that people back East imagined them to be. On the contrary, Custer claimed to have seen the Indian "as he is, and, so far as knowledge goes, as he has ever been, a savage in every sense of the word."[76] Custer took this disdain along with him as he and his 7th Cavalry Regiment left Fort Lincoln, Dakota Territory, in May 1876 to force the last of the free Indians to move onto a reservation.

The Indian resistance, led by Sitting Bull and the daring Cheyenne warrior Crazy Horse, came about partly because of Custer himself. His Black Hills expedition violated the U.S. government's own borderlines around the Great Sioux Reservation. According to the Fort Laramie treaty, no one except for the Sioux was "permitted to pass over, settle upon, or reside in the territory."[77] Worse still, Custer had ignored the far more significant boundaries that delineated the Indians' hunting grounds and their sacred space in the Black Hills. The fact that Custer found gold on Indian land only inflamed matters further. Gold miners rushed onto Sioux land, defacing the hills and insulting the Indians who responded by attacking them. The federal government did nothing to staunch the flow of trespassers. In fact, many in Washington urged more aggressive exploitation of the newly found gold fields, treaty or no treaty. In the words of one newspaper editorial, the provisions of the Fort Laramie treaty, in particular those guaranteeing the integrity of the Sioux reservation's borders, were "now pleaded as a barrier to the improvement and development of one of the richest and most fertile sections in America. What shall be done with these Indian dogs in our manger? They will not dig gold or let others do it."[78] Another newspaper went so far as to write a virtual obituary for the Native Americans and their way of life. "This is God's country," the editorial screeched:

> He peopled it with red men, and planted it with wild grasses, and permitted the white man to gain a foothold; and as the wild grasses disappear ... so the Indian disappears before the advances of the white man. Humanitarians may weep for [the Indian] and tell the wrongs he has suffered, but he is passing away. Their prayers, their entreaties, cannot change the law of nature; cannot arrest the causes which are carrying them on to their ultimate destiny—extinction. The American people need the country the Indians now occupy.[79]

The Native Americans' time had passed. It remained for the U.S. Army to convince them of it.

An undated photo of John Sitting Bull, survivor of the Battle of Little Bighorn, or Custer's Last Stand, in Montana. The famous chief once said of the reservation Indians, "You are fools to make yourselves slaves to a piece of fat bacon, some hard-tack, and a little sugar and coffee." It is no surprise that he led the resistance of Indians to reservation life. By the late 1880s, however, the Native American rebellion had all but been extinguished and the remaining territories organized into states. In 1887, the Dawes Act brought closure to the Indians' plight, forcing them to adopt "modern" culture, including land ownership and agriculture—to consider nature private property.

Custer's detachment was part of a larger operation involving forces under General Alfred Terry, General George Crook, and Colonel John Gibbon. Converging on the renegades led by Sitting Bull from three directions, the soldiers hoped to run the Indians down and either push them onto the reservation or destroy them. On June 25, 1876, troops under Custer's command located their quarry camped along the banks of the Little Big Horn River in Montana. Eager for battle and fame, Custer foolishly split his 900-man regiment into three parts and confidently announced to his commander, "We will go down and make a crossing and capture the village."[80]

Only after the operation had begun did the true situation reveal itself. The 7th Cavalry stumbled upon a massive encampment of well over 1,000 tepees, which translated into a fighting force of around 2,000 warriors. When he saw the village with his own eyes, Custer, in command of one of the three wings, dashed off a note to Captain Frederick Benteen urging him to "Come on. Big Village. Be quick. Bring packs."[81] He then gave the order to charge. When the day ended, Custer and all of the men under him had been killed; the other two commands, survivors of the most shocking and ignominious military defeat the nation had ever known, barely escaped.

Custer's Last Stand, as it came to be remembered, gave hope to many Native Americans from the Canadian border to Mexico. Defiant bands redoubled their efforts against both the reservation system and its underlying premise that Indian boundaries no longer mattered. Here and there, led by such renowned figures as the Apache guerilla Geronimo and the Nez Perce Chief Joseph, Indians openly rejected a future circumscribed by artificial lines drawn by outsiders. They also rejected abstract ideas about manifest destiny that, to Native Americans, legitimized wholesale theft.

Tragically, the Indian position became increasingly untenable. By the late 1880s, Native American resistance had been all but snuffed out and the last remaining portions of the old Louisiana Territory organized into states. Montana, North Dakota, and South Dakota entered the Union in 1889; Wyoming became the 44th state in 1890. Only Oklahoma, reserved since the 1830s for the Indian nations, remained separate as the nineteenth century came to a close. It would be granted statehood in 1907. Meanwhile, the land's original inhabitants were put onto a

Sioux tribespeople on a reservation in 1890. In a final effort to seek and snuff out the Indian custom of "Ghost Dancing," practiced by tribespeople for the purpose of spiritual renewal, government troops came across a Sioux village at Wounded Knee, South Dakota in December 1890. There, they came upon a group of villagers, who had been unnerved by the appearance of the soldiers and therefore armed. The soldiers fired on the villagers, killing 146. The event symbolized the end of the American frontier.

series of reservations spread out from the upper Mississippi to the Rocky Mountains. The last imaginary lines dictated by the abstraction known as the United States brought the long history of the Louisiana Territory nearer to its conclusion.

One last sad chapter, however, remained to be written. Not content with locking the Indians on reservations, the government moved to extinguish what remained of their culture and traditional ways. The 1887 Dawes Act compelled the Native Americans to accept "modern" forms of land ownership and agriculture; they were forced to view nature as private property. Under the act, each Indian head of household received 160 acres of farmland to call his own. "All our people," one Indian elder wrote, "were settling down in square gray houses, scattered here and there across this hungry land."[82]

For the most part this was true, but not all Indians were resigned to the slow strangulation of their culture. They resisted subjugation not with guns but with their souls. Through the 1880s, these "non-progressives," as they were labeled on the reservations, began seeking spiritual renewal.[83] They found it in the form of the Ghost Dance, a cult that promised a time when the ancient lifeways and a concrete relationship with nature would be restored. In an attempt to suppress the movement, the government sent troops out to the Sioux reservations in South Dakota in December 1890. Searching for the elusive Ghost Dancers, an army unit chanced upon the village of Wounded Knee. There they found a group of defiant young Indian men and a much larger group of women and children. Unnerved by the soldiers' presence, the men armed themselves and refused to surrender. History fails to record exactly whether it was a trooper or an Indian who fired the first shot, but in the ensuing melee, the soldiers shot at anything that moved. When the rifles fell silent, the army counted 146 Sioux villagers dead in the snow.

"Wounded Knee," historian Ronald Takaki has written, "violently symbolized the end of the frontier."[84] He might have said that it also ended a unique understanding of the land Native Americans cherished so deeply. As Frederick Jackson Turner declared, after 1890, the frontier closed. All of the previous ways of conceiving of the land had been eclipsed. Rather than seeing open space and natural relationships, the people who looked out across the Mississippi in the twentieth century saw an American heartland where "traditional values" meant the values of Thomas Jefferson. Modern observers shared Jefferson's dream of an "empire of liberty" bound together by an ideology of divinely ordained progress and arbitrary borders. More than nature, more than politics, the lines that cut through the old Louisiana Territory now defined abstractions—ideas about the country and its citizenry. With this final phase of the Louisiana Territory's development complete, the place faded into history and folklore, remembered vaguely by generations of schoolchildren as the land Thomas Jefferson bought, Lewis and Clark explored, and the Indians used to roam.

10

A Place
Remembered

Ever since Wounded Knee, the Louisiana Territory has slumbered. The memory of the place has remained a matter of local interest, but rarely has it entered into popular conversation. Of course, the twin anniversaries of the Louisiana Purchase and the Lewis and Clark expedition have generated some curiosity among average Americans about the territory and the ideological structure that became an integral part of it. With the commemoration of Thomas Jefferson's handiwork, the public has an opportunity to experience manifest destiny all over again. People living in what some call an "imperial" America, which dominates the world every bit as much as the European empires it gradually supplanted, have a chance to feel, however vicariously, a sense of divine mission, a sensation of transcendent national purpose.

The two hundredth anniversary of Louisiana's acquisition has produced a spate of books, most aimed at the general public, which claim to recount a time of heroism and adventure that exemplified the American spirit. Throughout the Great Plains region, from St. Louis to the Oregon coast, men and women are dressing up in period costumes and laboring with sore feet and aching backs to retrace at least short stretches of the ground Lewis and Clark covered. One such "expedition," put on by the National Park Service, promises to follow the Corps of Discovery's route "as nearly as possible" and "emphasize conservation, history, education, and reconciliation with Native Americans."[85] The Park Service portrays the adventure as a means by which the Louisiana Territory can be integrated into the story of a vibrant, progressive nation: "It will honor an emerging United States at the beginning of the nineteenth century, reveal the state of America at the beginning of the 21st century, and explore our future." Historical festivals range from Sacajawea Heritage Days in Salmon, Idaho, to the Lewis and Clark Goosefest in Pierre, South Dakota, which promises to celebrate Lewis and Clark as well as the annual goose migration.[86] Softened by a modern life of comfort and convenience, people leap at the chance to test themselves against men who seem to

A Lewis and Clark Trail marker, along U.S. Highway 12, in Idaho, around 2001. As the United States prepared for the bicentennial of the Louisiana Purchase and of Lewis and Clark's famous Corps of Discovery trek, the National Park Service announced an "expedition" along their famous route, one that would "emphasize conservation, history, education, and reconciliation with Native Americans."

embody the very essence of the American project—the expansion of liberty and justice outward into a savage, corrupt world—and thereby revive a sense of shared goals and direction.

For those unwilling to bear the actual burden of even a brief stint on the trails, technology has the virtual answer—a thundering, wide-screen IMAX motion picture that offers to put the audience in the thick of things with the Corps of Discovery as it rides rapids and climbs snowy peaks, all in surround-sound stereo. The film's makers assure people that they will be transported back in time to "the dawn of a nation" when men were "courageous in spirit and unyielding in their dedication to their mission." The advertisement continues, "Audiences will experience the danger and beauty of the unknown West as it unfolded before [the eyes] of Lewis and Clark."[87] As one reviewer has written, however, the movie presents such a "grandiose" view "on the advent of manifest destiny" that it serves as "less a history lesson than a set of commemorative postcards."[88]

It is unclear, at first glance, how the historical place and process that was the Louisiana Territory can be usefully integrated into a general understanding of how nations—and more specifically the arbitrary borders that define them—evolve from material to abstract divisions. One could rightfully ask what use might be made of Louisiana's story. The Louisiana Territory as a discrete, bounded space has been gone for over 150 years. The bold, dark lines that marked it out on nineteenth-century maps have long been erased. Of course, the territory makes cameo appearances in history textbooks and popular historical events such as those mentioned above, but the actual place vanished generations ago. The Louisiana Territory has some minor cultural significance as part of the national memory, but it has no function. It is, for all intents and purposes, defunct, unusable. It is tempting, therefore, to dismiss the place as having little to teach people about geographic change over time, especially in terms of arbitrary border formation.

Such a hasty and superficial assessment, however, misses the broader lessons of Louisiana's process of development. The territory, like other social, cultural, and political creations elsewhere in the world, was both a real and an imagined space. It had tangible existence in time—a natural state comprising prairies, mountains, rivers, and an array of living things. It also represented an imaginary complex, a set of ideas that gave it meaning.

Borders surrounded both the real and the fictional Louisiana Territory, arbitrary borders that shifted, dissolved, and rematerialized again and again. These boundaries changed along with the culture and politics at any given moment; they rose and fell in concert with their creators and their creators' agendas. What the Louisiana Territory meant, in other words, depended upon who was looking at it and why. Human eyes and minds determined the everyday reality of almost a million square miles of North America.

Just like the Mason-Dixon Line, the U.S.–Mexico border, the 17th Parallel, or the Iron Curtain, the Louisiana Territory became whatever its viewers wanted it to be. Like the other borderlines, those of Louisiana artificially divided a naturally unified space. Its boundaries, over the centuries, cut across a real landscape in the process of constructing an illusion.

Imaginary lines, arbitrary borders, continue to be drawn according to specific cultural, political, and ideological needs and desires. They continue to be laid over a natural world oblivious to their presence. Only their makers see them, but those who make them jealously defend them. The tensions, conflicts, and bloodshed that result from disagreements over what bordered spaces mean today are remarkably similar to those played out in the Louisiana Territory. The same rivalries and bitterness remain all too familiar in modern times. Around the globe, observers with hostile agendas define and redefine places, each observer seeing them his way and no other. One set of observers might view the land, from rainforests to deserts, in material-cultural terms. Another might see the same land through the filter of geopolitics, while yet another might conceive of it in terms of the nationalistic images and ideas it evokes. These premises often grow into fundamental disagreements that lead to oppression, injustice, and war. It was certainly the case during the life of the Louisiana Territory, and it remains so today.

Herein lies the value of learning the Louisiana Territory's story. As people seem likely to persist in fighting over imaginary places and shooting at each other across arbitrary borders, knowing how those places evolved and how those borders changed becomes a crucial exercise. This sort of knowledge can provide a vital tool for gaining a deeper understanding of the patterns of human interaction and behavior. To know a place is to know a people. This is perhaps the most valuable and timely lesson we can learn by seeing how other people at other times looked at the Louisiana Territory.

c. 11,000 B.C. The first humans arrive in what would become the Louisiana Territory.

1542 Francisco Vásquez de Coronado leads a Spanish expedition into the heart of North America. His journey takes him as far as modern Kansas.

1673 Jacques Marquette travels down the Mississippi from Lake Michigan as far as the Arkansas River. His trip establishes a French presence in the Mississippi Valley.

1682 Robert Cavalier, Sieur de La Salle, completes the navigation of the Mississippi begun by Marquette. In April, he reaches the mouth of the river, and claims the area for France. La Salle names the land Louisiana after the French king Louis XV.

1718 The city of New Orleans is founded.

1754–1763 France and Spain make war against Great Britain. The most important battles occur in North America, where the war is known as the French and Indian War.

1762 In order to keep it away from the British in case France loses the war, the French transfer Louisiana to Spain.

1763 The war between France and Britain ends; the British take possession of all French territory from the Appalachians to the Mississippi. Fearing trouble with Indians accustomed to French rule, the British draw a line down the crest of the Appalachians to separate the Indians from American colonists. The line soon becomes a hated and indefensible internal border known as the Proclamation Line.

1775–1783 The American Revolution is fought.

1783 The Paris Peace Treaty ends the revolution and confirms the independence of the United States. The western border of the new nation is set at the Mississippi, bringing it in direct contact with Spanish Louisiana.

1784 Fearful of American western settlement, Spain closes the Mississippi to American traffic.

1786 John Jay negotiates a deal to reopen the Mississippi. Seen as favoring Northeastern interests at the expense of Western farmers, the deal is rejected.

1795 With revolution and war in Europe, Spain relents and reopens the Mississippi. Pinckney's Treaty guarantees American river access and the right of deposit at New Orleans.

1801 Weary of administering Louisiana and intent on gaining the favor of Napoleon Bonaparte, Spain secretly transfers the colony back to France.

1803 Napoleon, planning to open an offensive against the British and nearing a defeat in his effort to put down the Haitian rebellion, sells Louisiana to the United States. Thomas Jefferson, who originally had sought to purchase just New Orleans, takes the rest of the territory as well when it was offered. The purchase costs the United States $15 million.

1763
Britian gains control of all lands from the Appalachian Mountains to the Mississippi River

1682
Robert Cavalier, Sieur La Salle, founds Louisiana as a French colony

1801
In a secret treaty, Spain transfers Louisiana back to Napoleon's France

1682

1801

1762
France transfers Louisiana to Spain

1783
The newly independent United States takes over former British territory, and establishes its border with Spanish America along the Mississippi

1804–1806 A survey party under the command of Meriwether Lewis and William Clark explores the Louisiana Territory as far as the Pacific Ocean. In conjunction with Zebulon Pike's expedition to the Ricky Mountains in 1806, the Lewis and Clark's expedition provides crucial data on the territory Jefferson purchased.

1821 The first state emerges out of the Louisiana Territory. Missouri enters the Union as a slave state in a compromise to avoid a fight over the extension of slavery into Louisiana. In an attempt to prevent future clashes over the issue, Congress draws a line at 30° 30′ and declares that all new territories and states above it will be admitted as free states; those below the line will enter as slave states.

1803
Thomas Jefferson's administration purchases Louisiana from France

1890
The traditional Indian conception of Louisiana is extinguished during the massacre at Wounded Knee, South Dakota

1821
Missouri becomes the first state carved out of Louisiana

1803

1890

1804–1806
Meriwether Lewis and William Clark explore the Louisiana Purchase territory as far as the Pacific Ocean

1846–1848
Victory in the Mexican War removes Louisiana's last foreign boundary, and eliminates the last remnant of the imperial vision of Louisiana's borders

1846–1848 The United States and Mexico fight a war over the border in Texas. The Treaty of Guadalupe Hidalgo ends the war and gives all of the far West to the U.S.

1854 The Missouri Compromise is effectively annulled with the passage of Stephen Douglas's Kansas-Nebraska Act. The act provides for the creation of two new territories out of Louisiana: Kansas and Nebraska. When time comes for statehood, the act leaves the issue of slavery up to the people in the territories, totally disregarding the Missouri Compromise Line.

1856 Pro-slavery and antislavery militia forces battle one another in Kansas in order to determine whether the state will enter the Union as a free or slave state.

1857 The Supreme Court officially erases the Missouri Compromise Line in its Dred Scott decision. The Court rules that no territory or state can prohibit slavery. All political remedies for the slavery problem are now exhausted.

1861–1865 The United States is torn in two over slavery. The resulting Civil War becomes the bloodiest conflict in American history. The old Louisiana Territory experiences the war as a vicious contest between guerilla bands.

1864 United States troops under the command of Colonel John Chivington massacre a peaceful group of Indians at Sand Creek in Colorado.

1867–1868 A pair of treaties result in the establishment of the Native American reservation system on the Great Plains. Not all Indians approve; many refuse to abandon their traditional ways of life.

1876 A large group of Sioux and Cheyenne, resisting confinement on reservations and angry over violation of the sacred Black Hills by miners, fight a federal force that includes George Armstrong Custer's 7th Cavalry Regiment. In June, at the Little Big Horn River, Custer and his command are wiped out in an ill-advised attack against the main Indian camp.

1890 The Indian Wars and the last vestiges of the ancient ways of looking at the Louisiana Territory end with the massacre of Indians at the village of Wounded Knee in South Dakota.

Chapter 1

1. Jack McLaughlin, *To His Excellency Thomas Jefferson: Letters to a President.* New York: Avon Books, 1991, pp. 10–11.
2. Ibid., pp. 11–12.
3. Ibid., p. 13.
4. Ibid., p. 63.
5. Ibid., p. 64.
6. Robert W. Tucker and David C. Hendrickson, *Empire of Liberty: the Statecraft of Thomas Jefferson.* New York: Oxford University Press, 1990, p. ix.

Chapter 2

7. Douglas G. Brinkley, *The Mississippi and the Making of a Nation: From the Louisiana Purchase to Today.* Washington, D.C.: National Geographic Society, 2002, p. 9.
8. David Rockwell, *The Nature of North America: A Handbook to a Continent—Rocks, Plants, and Animals.* New York: Berkley Books, 1998, pp. 87–89.
9. Bernard DeVoto, ed. *The Journals of Lewis and Clark.* Boston: Houghton Mifflin, 1953, p. 95.
10. Rockwell, *Nature of North America,* p. 209.
11. Robert McCracken Peck, *Land of the Eagle: A Natural History of North America.* New York: Summit Books, 1990, p. 126.
12. Rockwell, *Nature of North America,* p. 161.
13. Peck, *Land of the Eagle,* p. 126.
14. Ibid.
15. Rockwell, *Nature of North America,* p. 90.
16. Brinkley, *The Mississippi,* p. 11.
17. Peck, *Land of the Eagle,* p. 130.
18. Ibid., p. 126.
19. DeVoto, *Journals of Lewis and Clark,* p. 103.
20. Ibid., p. 102.

Chapter 3

21. Geoffrey Turner, *Indians of North America.* New York: Sterling Publishing Company, 1979, p. 8.
22. Ibid., p.10.
23. Gary B. Nash, *Red, White, and Black: The Peoples of Early America.* Edgewood Cliffs, NJ: Prentice Hall, Inc., 1982, p. 9.

24. Carl Waldman, *Atlas of the North American Indian.* New York: Facts On File, 1985, p. 40.
25. Ted Morgan, *Wilderness at Dawn: The Settling of the North American Continent.* New York: Simon and Schuster, 1993, p. 35.
26. Tom Holm, "Warriors and Warfare," *Encyclopedia of North American Indians.* http://college.hmco.com/history/readerscomp/taind/html/na_142200_warriorsandw.htm Online. 6/23/2004.
27. Nash, *Red, White, and Black,* p. 26.
28. Jon Manchip White, *Everyday Life of the North American Indians.* New York: Dorsett Press, 1979, p. 49.

Chapter 4

29. James Axtell, *Beyond 1492: Encounters in Colonial North America.* New York: Oxford University Press, 1992, p. 249.
30. J.H. Elliot, *The Old World and the New, 1492–1650.* New York: Cambridge University Press, 1970, p. 60.
31. Ibid.
32. Brinkley, *The Mississippi,* p. 11.
33. Morgan, *Wilderness at Dawn,* p. 205.
34. Joseph Harriss, "Westward Ho!" Smithsonian (April 2003), p. 104.
35. Francis Jennings, *The Invasion of America: Indians, Colonialism, and the Cant of Conquest.* New York W. W. Norton and Company, 1975, p. 101.
36. Reuben Gold Thwaites, *France in America: 1497–1763.* Westport, CT: Greenwood Press, reprint, 1970, pp. 273–274.

Chapter 5

37. Marc Egnal, *A Mighty Empire: The Origins of the American Revolution.* Ithaca, NY: Cornell University Press, 1988, p. 6.
38. Ibid., p. 12.
39. "Treaty of Peace With Great Britain, September 3, 1783," *Documents of American History,* ed. Henry Steele Commager. New York: Appleton-Century-Crofts, 1958, p. 118.
40. Ezra Stiles, "The United States Elevated to Glory and Honour," in *Major Problems in American Foreign Policy, Volume I: To 1914,* ed. Thomas G. Paterson. Lexington,

Massachusetts: D.C. Heath and
Company, 1989, pp. 38–39.

41. "The Pinckney Treaty, October 27, 1795,"
in *Documents of American History*, 168.

42. Tucker and Hendrickson, *Empire of
Liberty*, p. 104.

43. Harriss, "Westward Ho!" p. 104.

Chapter 6

44. "Jefferson on the Importance of New
Orleans: Letter to Robert R. Livingston,
April 18, 1802," *Documents of American
History*, pp. 189–190.

45. John Leland, "Why America Sees the
Silver Lining," *New York Times*,
13 June 2004, WK 1.

46. Merrill Peterson, ed., *The Portable
Thomas Jefferson*. New York: Penguin
Books, 1975, 494.

47. Harriss, "Westward Ho!" p. 105.

48. Ibid., p. 106.

49. "Napoleon on the Sale of Louisiana,
1803," in *Major Problems in American
Foreign Policy*, pp. 111–112.

50. Arthur DeConde, *A History of
American Foreign Policy*. New York:
Charles Scribner's Sons, 1971, p. 83.

51. Peterson, *Portable Thomas Jefferson*,
p. 497.

52. Bernard DeVoto, ed., *The Journals of
Lewis and Clark*. New York: Houghton
Mifflin, 1953, p. 8.

53. Ibid., pp. 8–9.

54. Ibid., p. 36.

55. Ibid., p. 95.

56. Ibid., p. 28.

57. Ibid., p. 279.

Chapter 7

58. LeRoy R. Hafen, ed., *Mountain Men &
Fur Traders of the Far West*. Lincoln:
University of Nebraska Press, 1972,
p. xviii.

59. Merrill D. Peterson, *The Great
Triumvirate: Webster, Clay, and Calhoun*.
New York: Oxford University Press, 1987,
p. 60.

60. The state of Louisiana had been created
out of something called the Territory of
Orleans, which had been established as a
separate entity in 1805. For seven years,
from 1805 to 1812, Orleans functioned as
an independent territory, complete with
its own governor. Thus, strictly speaking,
Missouri was the first state to emerge
from the Louisiana Territory.

61. Peterson, *Portable Thomas Jefferson*,
p. 568.

62. "John L. O'Sullivan on Manifest Destiny,
1939," *Major Problems in American
Foreign Policy*, pp. 255–256.

Chapter 8

63. "The Kansas-Nebraska Act, May 30,
1854," in *Documents in American History*,
p. 332.

64. David M. Potter, *The Impending Crisis,
1848–1861*. New York: Harper & Row,
1963, p. 207.

65. "*Dred Scott v. Sandford*, 19 Howard 393,
1857," in *Documents in American History*,
p. 345.

66. Emory M. Thomas, *The Confederate
Nation, 1861–1865*. New York: History
Book Club, 1993, p. 247.

67. James McPherson, *Battle Cry of Freedom:
The Civil War Era*. New York: Oxford
University Press, 1988, p. 292.

Chapter 9

68. Robert M. Utley, *The Indian Frontier of
the American West, 1846–1890*.
Albuquerque: University of New Mexico
Press, 1984, p. 92.

69. Ibid., p. 93.

70. Ibid., p. 35.

71. "Removal of the Southern Indians to
Indian Territory, December 7, 1835," in
Documents in American History, p. 260.

72. Utley, *Indian Frontier*, p. 76.

73. Ibid., p. 178.

74. Ibid., pp. 178–179.

75. Stephen Longstreet, *Indian Wars of the
Great Plains*. New York: Indian Head
Books, 1993, p. 181.

76. James Welch, *Killing Custer: The Battle of
the Little Big Horn and the Fate of the
Plains Indians*. New York: W.W. Norton
and Company, 1994, p. 130.

77. Evan S. Connell, *Son of the Morning Star:
Custer and the Little Big Horn*. New York:
HarperPerennial, 1991, p. 238.

78. Ibid.

79. Ibid., p. 241.

80. Ibid., p. 278.

81. Ibid.

82. Utley, *Indian Frontier*, p. 230.
83. Ibid., p. 234.
84. Ronald Takaki, *A Different Mirror: A History of Multicultural America*. Boston: Little, Brown and Company, 1993, p. 231.

Chapter 10

85. "Lewis and Clark Bicentennial Celebration," *Parks and Recreation* (March 2001). http://articles.finadarti-cles.com/p/articles/mi_m1145/is_3_36/ai _72868381 Online. 6/23/2004.

86. See Lewis and Clark National Historic Trail. http://www.nps.gov.lecl/Events/festival/htm.
87. "Lewis and Clark: Great Journey West (IMAX)," http://www.bifmoviezone.com/filmsearch/movies/?uniq=215 Online. 6/265/2004.
88. Nick Rutigliano, "Bigger They Come," *The Village Voice* (August 2002). http://www.villagevoice.com/issues/0233/rutigliano.php Online. 6/26/2004.

PRIMARY SOURCES

Commager, Henry Steele, ed. *Documents of American History*. 6th ed. New York: Appleton Century-Crofts, 1958.

DeVoto, Bernard, ed. *The Journals of Lewis and Clark*. Boston: Houghton Mifflin Company, 1953.

Paterson, Thomas G., ed. *Major Problems in American Foreign Policy, Volume I: To 1914*. 2 Vols. Lexington, MA: D.C. Heath and Company, 1989.

Peterson, Merrill D., ed. *The Portable Thomas Jefferson*. New York: Penguin Books, 1975.

SECONDARY SOURCES

Axtell, James. *Beyond 1492: Encounters in Colonial North America*. New York: Oxford University Press, 1992.

Brinkley, Douglas G. *The Mississippi and the Making of a Nation: From the Louisiana Purchase to Today*. Washington, D.C.: National Geographic Society, 2002.

Connell, Evan S. *Son of the Morning Star: Custer and the Little Big Horn*. New York: HarperPerennial, 1984.

DeConde, Alexander. *A History of American Foreign Policy*. 2nd. ed. New York: Charles Scribner's Sons, 1971.

Egnal, Marc. *A Mighty Empire: The Origins of the America Revolution*. Ithaca, NY: Cornell University Press, 1988.

Emory, Thomas M. *The Confederate Nation, 1861–1865*. New York: History Book Club, 1993.

Harriss, Joseph. "Westward Ho!" *Smithsonian*, April 2003.

Holm, Tom. "Warriors and Warfare." *Encyclopedia of North American Indians*. http://college.hmco.com/history/readerscomp/naind/html/na_04220_warriorsandw.htm Online. April 15, 2004.

Josephy, Alvin, Jr. *The Civil War in the American West*. New York: Random House, 1991.

Kennedy, Roger G. *Mr. Jefferson's Lost Cause: Land, Farmers, Slavery, and the Louisiana Purchase.* New York: Oxford University Press, 2003.

Kinzer, Stephen. "American Prairie Overlooked No More," *New York Times,* June 24, 2004, A14.

Krech, Shepard, III. *The Ecological Indian: Myth and History.* New York: W. W. Norton, 1999.

Leland, John. "Why America Sees the Silver Lining," *New York Times,* June 13, 2004, WK1.

Longstreet, Stephen. *Indian Wars of the Great Plains.* New York: Indian Head Books, 1970.

McLaughlin, Jack. *To His Excellency Thomas Jefferson: Letters to a President.* New York: Avon Books, 1991.

McPherson, James M. *Battle Cry of Freedom: The Civil War Era.* New York: W.W. Norton, 1988.

Mitchell, John G. "Change of Heartland: America's Rural Interior Searches for New Horizons." *National Geographic,* May 2004, 2.

Morgan, Ted. *Wilderness at Dawn: The Settling of the North American Continent.* New York: Simon & Schuster, 1993.

Nash, Gary B. *Red, White, and Black: The People of Early America.* Englewood Cliffs, NJ: Prentice-Hall, 1982.

Peck, Robert McCracken. *Land of the Eagle: A Natural History of North America.* New York: Summit Books, 1990.

Potter, David M. *The Impending Crisis, 1848–1861.* New York: Harper Torchbooks, 1976.

Rockwell, David. *The Nature of North America: A Handbook to the Continent—Rocks, Plants and Animals.* New York: Berkley Books, 1998.

Takaki, Ronald. *A Different Mirror: A History of Multicultural America.* Boston: Little Brown, 1993.

Thwaites, Reuben Gold. *France in America, 1497–1763.* New York: Harper & Brothers Publishers, 1905; reprint, Westport, Connecticut: Greenwood Press, 1970.

Tucker, Robert W. and David C. Hendrickson. *Empire of Liberty: The Statecraft of Thomas Jefferson.* New York: Oxford University Press, 1990.

Turner, Geoffrey. *Indians of North America.* New York: Sterling, 1992.

Utley, Robert M. *The Indian Frontier of the American West, 1846–1890.* Albuquerque: University of New Mexico Press, 1984.

Waldman, Carl. *Atlas of the North American Indian.* New York: Facts-On-File, 1985.

Welch, James. *Killing Custer: The Battle of the Little Big Horn and the Fate of the Plains Indians.* New York: W.W. Norton and Company, 1994.

White, Jon Manchip. *Everyday Life of the North American Indians.* New York: Dorsett Press, 1979.

Ambrose, Stephen. *Undaunted Courage: Meriwether Lewis, Thomas Jefferson, and the Opening of the American West.* New York: Simon & Schuster, 2001.

Anderson, Fred. *Crucible of War: The Seven Years' War and the Fate of Empire in British North America, 1754–1766.* New York: Alfred A. Knopf, 2000.

Burstein, Andrew. *Sentimental Democracy: The Evolution of America's Romantic Self-image.* New York: Hill and Wang, 1999.

Caruso, John Anthony. *The Mississippi Valley Frontier: The Age of French Exploration and Settlement.* Indianapolis, IN: Bobbs-Merrill, 1966.

Eccles, John William. *France in America.* New York: Harper Row, 1972.

Lowie, Robert. *Indians of the Plains.* Omaha: University of Nebraska Press, 1982.

Rice, Earle. *Life Among the Plains Indians.* San Diego: Lucent Books, 1998.

Saum, Lewis O. *The Popular Mood of Pre-Civil War America.* Westport, CT: Greenwood Press, 1980.

Uschan, Michael V. *Westward Expansion.* San Diego: Lucent Books, 2001.

West, Elliot. *The Contested Plains: Indians, Goldseekers, and the Rush to Colorado.* Lawrence: University Press of Kansas, 2000.

page:

3: © Bettman/CORBIS
7: © CORBIS
12: Associated Press, The Pioneer of Bemidji, Minn.
17: Associated Press, AP
24: Library of Congress No. LC-USZ62-86381
30: Library of Congress No. LC-USZ62-37993
43: © Getty Images
46: Library of Congress No. LC-USZ62-96380
57: Bettman/CORBIS
62: © Getty Images

69: © Getty Images
80: Library of Congress No. LC-DIG-ewpbh-00882
83: Library of Congress No. LC-DIG-ewpbh-03067
84: Library of Congress No. LC-DIG-ewpbh-00788
94: Library of Congress No. LC-DIG-ewpbh-01012
97: Associated Press, AP
99: Library of Congress, No. LC UZ62-54813
104: © Connie Ricca/CORBIS

frontis: ©Bettman/CORBIS
cover: ©Bettman/CORBIS

John Davenport holds a Ph.D. from the University of Connecticut and currently teaches at Corte Madera School in Portola Valley, California. Davenport is the author of several other books, including biographies of the Muslim leader Saladin and the writer C.S. Lewis. He lives in San Carlos, California, with his wife, Jennifer, and his two sons, William and Andrew.

George J. Mitchell served as chairman of the peace negotiations in Northern Ireland during the 1990s. Under his leadership, an historic accord, ending decades of conflict, was agreed to by the governments of Ireland and the United Kingdom and the political parties in Northern Ireland. In May 1998, the agreement was overwhelmingly endorsed by a referendum of the voters of Ireland, North and South. Senator Mitchell's leadership earned him worldwide praise and a Nobel Peace Prize nomination. He accepted his appointment to the U.S. Senate in 1980. After leaving the Senate, Senator Mitchell joined the Washington, D.C. law firm of Piper Rudnick, where he now practices law. Senator Mitchell's life and career have embodied a deep commitment to public service and he continues to be active in worldwide peace and disarmament efforts.

James I. Matray is professor of history and chair at California State University, Chico. He has published more than forty articles and book chapters on U.S.-Korean relations during and after World War II. Author of *The Reluctant Crusade: American Foreign Policy in Korea, 1941–1950* and *Japan's Emergence as a Global Power*, his most recent publication is *East Asia and the United States: An Encyclopedia of Relations Since 1784*. Matray also is international columnist for the *Donga Ilbo* in South Korea.